THE
Storyteller's
DEVOTIONAL
VOLUME TWO

THE
Storyteller's
DEVOTIONAL

VOLUME TWO

CLIFTON WEST

Some instances of paraphrased dialogue in the book are combined with actual quoted scripture. In those cases, the scripture portion is in single quotation marks, followed immediately by the scripture reference in parenthesis.

HGR
Editorial Services
Homer G. Rhea, Managing Editor
Donna Rhea Smith, Layout and Cover Design
homer8238@gmail.com

ISBN 9798404543995

Dedicated to my dear parents, Earl and Marie West, in whose arms I heard my very first stories. At the dinner table, in a fishing boat, by the fireplace, and in the family car, your stories have shaped my life like no other. And for this, I will always be grateful.

And a special thanks to Homer G. Rhea, managing editor, whose expertise and know-how calm a writer's nerves. There's no sweating bullets after handing you the manuscript. I can breathe easily, knowing you're in my corner.

Table of Contents

PART TWO: PLACES TO GO

Table of Contents

PART THREE: PURPOSE TO FULFILL

TOPICAL INDEX

These are written that you may believe that Jesus is the Messiah, the Son of God, and that by believing you may have life in his name.
(JOHN 20:31 NIV)

Preface

Stories are the foundation of life. From cave drawings of ancient civilizations to etched records on modern-day monuments, stories communicate who we are, where we have been, and where we are going.

It is my pleasure to offer you ninety spellbinding stories in the newest volume of *The Storyteller's Devotional.* You will laugh. You will cry. You will meet new people and travel to new places. And when your journey is complete, you will live life on purpose, just like Jesus.

The Storyteller's Devotional Volume Two is divided into three major sections:

Part One: "People to Know" introduces you to patriarchs of the past and heroes of the present. You will hear the prayerful plea of a Shunamite woman and listen to the soulful music of a saxophone player in the Bayou. You will witness the transformation of a Harley Davidson biker and be transformed by the testimony of a teenage boy with cerebral palsy.

Part Two: "Places to Go" invites you to walk the southern rim of the Grand Canyon. Listen to Jesus share his heart on Mount Hermon and share his resurrection story on the Emmaus Road. Join me for moments of inspiration in the local coffee shop, and watch David struggle with despair at a place called Ezel Rock.

Part Three: "Purpose to Fulfill" raises you to a higher plane, from the mundane to the miraculous. Understand the real meaning of life as you learn from the examples of Jeremiah the prophet, Zechariah the priest, and Jesus Christ, the promised Messiah. Soar with Canadian geese, step into the empty tomb with Simon Peter, and hold your breath as a courageous man crosses Niagara Falls on a tightrope 160 feet in the air.

Read the story. Become the story. Tell the story.

—Clifton West

PART ONE

People to Know

ONE

Big Mac

The guttural snarl of a motorcycle interrupted my afternoon nap. It sounded like a biker drove up in the front yard. Before I could get up on my feet, he started pounding on the door. I tiptoed to the window and looked out. There he stood on the porch with his head wrapped in a red bandana. His scraggly beard hid his face, and his leather jacket screamed Hells Angels. Reluctantly, I opened the door. "May I help you?"

He had a gold tooth like a Wild West rambler in a Clint Eastwood movie. "You don't remember me, do you?" He cleared his throat and spit a loogie over the hedge bushes.

"No. Have we met before?"

He took off his shades so I could get a better look. His eyebrows looked like thorn bushes. "Mac Stetson," he said. "Remember? I took you up in my airplane."

Then it hit me like a blast from the past. "Wow! Big Mac, I didn't recognize you. It's been what, twenty years?"

"Thirty," he corrected me. "I saw your name on the church sign down the road. Thought I'd say hello."

"Yes, I'm preaching tonight. You're welcome to come."

He laughed like an escapee who'd been invited to the warden's house. "Not a chance. I quit church after Deanna left, and I ain't going back anytime soon." (I wondered what had happened. The last time I saw him, he was a deacon in the church.) "I'd like to sit down with you though," he said. "Coffee after church?"

"Sure."

"I'm two and a half miles past the school, on the left. You can't miss it. My bike will be in the drive." His muffler growled all the way down the road as he sped away. I could smell where he'd been standing—alcohol, leather, and something that's probably illegal.

After church, I changed into some jeans and a pullover, then grabbed my leather jacket. At least I'd look the part at Mac's house.

17

When I arrived, three bikes were in his driveway. I was outnumbered. The porch was littered with beer bottles and empty pork and beans cans. Music blared inside, and it wasn't Lauren Daigle or Hillsong. I tried to think of a Bible verse before I knocked on the door, but my mind went numb. I felt like a church mouse in a snake pit.

A redhead opened the door, holding a beer and a cigarette in the same hand. "Come in," she said, and hugged me before I got both feet in the door. "The preacher's here," she shouted.

Mac was sitting at the head of the table with a biker dude on his left. He waved me in with a half-eaten slice of pizza. As he talked around the food in his mouth, he said, "Preacher, this is Shorty. Shorty, this is the preacher I told you about." Shorty nodded and I hung my jacket on the back of the chair.

Mac laid the pizza down and went full throttle into his story: Deanna was a cheat, the church was a bunch of hypocrites, and God didn't care a hill of beans. If he did, why did he let their fourteen-year-old son die? The three bikers sat around the table and glared at me like I had all the answers.

"Mac, I'm sorry your wife left, I'm sorry your son died, and I'm really sorry it feels like God is a million miles away."

"If there is a God," Shorty piped in.

I looked straight into Mac's eyes and could tell he knew what I knew—there is a God, but sometimes it doesn't feel like it. "We live in a messed up world," I said. "I can't explain why things happen like they do. But life is a whole lot easier to handle when you've got Jesus in your heart than when you don't." Mac batted away a tear, ate his pizza, and talked about Harleys the rest of the night.

The next evening, Mac did what he said he'd never do again. He came to church to listen to an old friend talk about the one Friend who loves you no matter what. Several years have passed since then. Mac is still without his wife and son, but the last time I saw him, he was grinning with a gold tooth and wearing a jacket advertising "Jesus Loves Harleys."

"Return to Me," says the LORD of hosts,
"and I will return to you."
(ZECHARIAH 1:3)

TWO

The Family Feud

They were twin brothers but were as different as night and day. One took after his dad. The other was a mamma's boy. The oldest was as hairy as a bear, wore camouflage, and sported *Field & Stream* magazine. The younger was the family chef, wore kitchen aprons, and subscribed to *Southern Cooking*. Esau and Jacob.

You might as well say Dr. Jekyll and Mr. Hyde or Hatfield and McCoy. Have two brothers ever been so different from each other? Yet they had one thing in common. They both wanted a blessing from their dying father.

According to their custom, the blessing belonged to the oldest son, but the younger set out to steal it. It was a scheme worthy of *Mission Impossible*. Jacob listened to his mother's advice on the covert recorder: "This message will self-destruct in five seconds." She was the lead instigator and the chief makeup artist. Rebecca disguised Jacob to look like (and smell like) Esau. Goat's hair—check. Deer scent—check. Camouflage—check. Savory stew—check.

The stage was set. Esau was in the woods hunting wild game. Blind Isaac was propped up in his bed, feeble and frail. Rebekah hid in the hallway and watched through the crack in the door. Jacob stood by his father's bed, shaking in his sandals. He lowered his chin and tried to speak in base tones, but his tenor voice couldn't quite pull it off.

Isaac was suspicious. He sniffed the air and caught whiffs of cedar wood and pine needles. "Come closer, my son." Jacob held his breath and shuffled forward. Isaac felt the goat's hair on the smooth of Jacob's neck and was satisfied. Rebekah closed her eyes and let out a sigh.

Isaac pronounced the blessing: "You will rule over your brothers, and they will kneel at your feet. Anyone who curses you will be cursed; anyone who blesses you will be blessed" (Genesis 27:29 CEV).

Jacob exited the room and gave his mother a high five. They pulled it off. Just as the celebration started, Esau waltzed through the back door with a pot full of stew. He strutted into Isaac's room, smiling like a grill master. Jacob and his mother hid their balloons and confetti and decided to party later. You can imagine what happened that night when it all hit the fan. Esau was enraged. Jacob was in danger.

It's a sad story of betrayal and deception. The truth is, every family member operated out of selfishness.

Isaac determined to bless Esau, even though God had said the older would serve the younger (Genesis 25:23). Esau's anger wasn't his biggest problem. He was immoral and godless (Hebrews 12:16). Rebekah deceived her blind husband with an underhanded scheme that would unravel any marriage. And Jacob flat-out lied to his dad, more than once, all for financial gain.

Each one lived their way instead of God's way, and it splintered the whole family. Jacob ran away and didn't come back for twenty years. Esau married two heathen women in spite of his parent's wishes. Rebekah's last recorded words are, "I am weary of my life" (Genesis 27:46). And the next time we see Isaac in the Bible, he's in the family cemetery (Genesis 49:31).

There's a better way to live. Jesus told us how—prefer one another.

"Do to others whatever you would like them to do to you."
(MATTHEW 7:12 NLT)

THREE

Albert in Overalls

The house smelled old and musty, the furniture was 1970s, and the old carpet was paper thin. But the fragrant love I found there was as fresh as the autumn breeze blowing through the kitchen window.

"Her snoring doesn't bother me," Albert said. "It means she's still alive." His mouth never stopped moving even when he stopped talking. His dentures soaked in a cup of bubbles on the TV tray. "We've been married fifty-two years," he said as he rocked his jaw back and forth like a pendulum. "And I love her more now than ever." He looked at his wife the same way I look at mine—with an enduring affection that neither time nor tragedy can diminish.

His pastor and I dropped by, on the way to lunch, to have a quick prayer for his wife. I didn't know we'd hang around for an hour listening to an old man talk about a new romance, but we did, and not a minute of it was wasted.

Her twin bed was in the dining room, not far from the table. We sat within arm's reach in chairs that creaked when we shifted our weight. He brushed hair out of her eyes and told us his story. "We fell in love and got married two days before I went off to war."

"Two days?" I chuckled. "Not much of a honeymoon."

He grinned. "Says who? We drove thirteen miles across the county line in a borrowed car, then ate BBQ sandwiches under the stars while we sat on the hood. The only motel around was a little hole-in-the-wall called Special's. We stayed in room number nine, so I told her I wanted nine kids."

I laughed again. "What did she think about that?"

"She hugged me around the neck and said, 'Then we best get started.'"

That old man was a hoot. I liked him from the time he opened the door and invited us in. He wore bibbed overalls with no shirt underneath, wool socks that didn't match, and a full beard that was Santa Claus white. His wife looked like Granny from the old TV show *The Beverly Hillbillies.* She slept the whole time we were there, but I felt like I knew her just the same.

"I love her," he said, "but I'll never love her as much as she's loved me." (I raised my eyebrows.) "You see, I was a rambler, a drunk, and a bar fight waiting to happen. She got me out of the drunk tank more than once. I'd promise to straighten up and go to church with her, but I never did." He patted her on the back of the hand with an appreciation that went beyond skin deep.

"Before she got sick, I'd find her kneeling right there in prayer every morning." He pointed to the corner. It was her prayer place. A simple chair sat against wood paneling. The seat cushion was stained with tears. On one wall hung a picture of praying hands. On the other wall hung a funeral home calendar with handwritten notes on each day.

His voice quivered as he told us about the calendar. "She has stacks of these in the bedroom, going back for years. She kept a record of her prayers, counting the days before I gave my heart to the Lord."

He walked over to the corner, pulled the thumbtack, and flipped back a few pages. Then he pointed to a date and handed it to me. The note was written in red. It said, "Albert got saved today." It was written on April the first.

"So you got saved on April Fool's Day?"

"I'm living proof that God saves fools," he chuckled.

I counted on my fingers: May, June, July, August, September, October, November. "Seven months."

"Yep. Next week will be my first sober Thanksgiving for as long as I can remember. And I've got so much to be thankful for. I've got a praying wife, and we both serve a prayer answering God. What more could a fellow want?"

After we left his house, I thought about it. His wife is not the only one with a prayer calendar. God has one too, but his calendar includes the answer dates. If your answer hasn't arrived yet, it may be on the next page. Don't worry, God circled it before you said Amen.

"I will go ahead and answer their prayers!"
(ISAIAH 65:24 NLT)

FOUR

Ten Brothers, One Savior

Ten brothers stood side by side with their backs against the wall, not a one of them brave enough to lift his chin. Their shepherds' robes looked like hand-me-downs compared to the Egyptians' ritzy tunics. They stared at their dirty feet on the marble floors in Joseph's palace and felt like backwoods boys in the gallery of the rich.

Reuben needed some nail clippers. Simeon needed a haircut. Judah needed a bar of soap. Issachar, Zebulon, and Asher needed Right Guard, Old Spice, and Listerine, in no particular order. They were a motley crew.

Fingers fidgeted, eyes darted, and sweat beaded. They stood shoulder to shoulder, guilt-ridden and red-handed, like felons in a lineup at police headquarters. Let me describe them to you from oldest to youngest: thief, cheat, swindler, liar, crook, thug, bandit, scoundrel, rascal, and lowlife. What a band of brothers.

Famine had ravished Canaan, so Jacob sent ten of his sons to Egypt to buy food. They had no way of knowing the brother they pawned away was in control of the storehouses. Joseph knew them right off, but they didn't recognize him. Why would they? He wore Egyptian clothes, lived in an Egyptian palace, spoke the Egyptian language, and ruled Egyptian servants. They had no idea that the Jewish blood coursing through his veins was from their father, Jacob.

"You are spies!" (Genesis 42:9 NLT) Joseph said through an interpreter. He played charades with them until he knew their heart. They couldn't weasel out of the trap he'd set for them.

They huddled together and hashed out their predicament. "Clearly we are being punished because of what we did to Joseph long ago" (Genesis 42:21 NLT).

Joseph heard every word they said, and it took him back to that dreadful day they sold him as a slave. His emotions got the best of him, and he had to turn his face away so they wouldn't see his tears. He heard every whisper and understood their lingo.

He knew everything about them. Reuben was the strongest, and Simeon was the slyest. Levi could sing well, and Naphtali couldn't sing at all. Gad had a lazy eye, and Dan had a missing tooth. He also knew they had one more brother, left-handed and left behind. The charade would last until he laid his eyes on Benjamin.

A few days later Joseph sent them off with provisions for their family, knowing they'd be back soon enough. And Benjamin, his closest brother, would be with them when they returned.

The day arrived. Eleven brothers trembled before the "cruel" proprietor of Egypt. Their stomachs were empty; their minds, full of fear. Joseph surprised them when he sat them at the banquet table according to their age. They thought the gods of Egypt had their number. (In reality, Joseph had their backs.) Head-scratching and finger-biting spread around the table. They were nervous but had no reason to be. Joseph had forgiven them, but they didn't know it yet.

When Joseph saw Benjamin, his emotions gushed like a river crashing over a dam. He sprinted to the lavatory, broke down, and wept. "After washing his face, he came back out, keeping himself under control" (Genesis 43:31 NLT).

The time finally came when Joseph could no longer hold back. "Out, all of you!" (Genesis 45:1 NLT). He ordered every Egyptian out of the room so he could reveal himself to his brothers. As soon as they left, he removed his headdress and burst into tears.

"I am Joseph!" he said with all the emotion of a Shakespearean hero. No interpreter needed. No translation necessary. He spoke to their hearts in their hometown dialect. "I am your brother Joseph."

When I see Joseph reveal himself to his brothers, weeping on their necks and embracing them with tender love, I see Jesus. Isn't that what he did for us on the cross? He held nothing back. He spoke our language. He identified with our guilt. And in spite of all our horrible deeds in the past, he loves us like there's no tomorrow.

The best part of this story is not the provisions in the storehouse during a time of famine; it's the revelation that our heavenly "Joseph" loves us the most when we deserve it the least.

His brothers were speechless!
(GENESIS 45:3 NLT)

FIVE

The Movie Director

*M*iriam hid in a small clump of date palms, squatting beneath a canopy of thick, leafy foliage. It wasn't the first time she'd played this game. She was the chameleon champion among the Hebrew slaves. Hide-and-seek was her favorite pastime. So when her mother floated baby Moses in a basket among the reeds (Exodus 2:3) and asked big sister to keep a sharp eye, Miriam was as comfy as a swamp cat in a thicket.

Miriam was in perfect position to scope out Pharaoh's daughter, but she wasn't the only one with prying eyes. Jochebed watched Miriam from a distance, Pharaoh's daughter spied Moses in the shallows, Moses glared at sunlight through holes in the basket, and all the while God surveilled the whole scene from the Director's chair, just like he's done from the beginning of time.

"Providence on the Riverbank—take one."

The Divine Director motions for Pharaoh's daughter to enter the water's edge. At the same time, he signals angels to float the basket where the young princess will find it (soft music). A single bird soars in the open sky. Pharaoh's daughter, flanked on both sides by handmaidens, wades knee-deep into the Nile River (camera shot of rippling water). They giggle and gossip about cute merchant men and tanned temple guards. Overheated by the midday sun, the princess ties her hair up and splashes cool water in her face. Aha! (dramatic music). She spots the woven basket in the shallows and sends a servant to fetch it.

Jochebed bites a lip. Miriam raises an eyebrow. Moses sheds a tear. But God nods in approval. He's got the script in his lap, and everything is going according to his plan.

Since God is the director, he decides that Pharaoh's daughter will have compassion on the Hebrew baby instead of killing it. He also choreographs the meeting between Miriam and the princess.

God pushes Miriam out of the shadows of the palm trees and into the limelight. God connects the dots—Miriam to Pharaoh's daughter to Jochebed to Moses.

God planned the whole thing: the Exodus, the Passover, and the Red Sea crossing. He also planned the Virgin Birth, the Crucifixion, and the Resurrection.

Bible stories sometimes read like fairytales, but it really happened. The great consolation is that the same God who designed Israel's history is the one who decides your destiny. "The LORD directs the steps of the godly. He delights in every detail of their lives" (Psalm 37:23 NLT).

Just because things don't work out according to your plan doesn't mean they're not working out according to his plan. And his plan is the best plan. "God's way is perfect" (Psalm 18:30 NLT).

So the next time you're in a pinch, try not to worry about a thing. The Divine Director sits in his chair, just above you, and orchestrates your life. If at any moment things go awry, he's got a bullhorn and an army of angels to get it back on track.

"Calm Nerves and Peace of Mind—take two."

For as the heavens are higher than the earth,
So are My ways higher than your ways.
(ISAIAH 55:9)

SIX

Myles the Music Man

The New Orleans sun baked the French Quarter as the smell of fresh beignets filled the air. On the concrete curb sat an old man on a plastic crate that creaked beneath his portly weight. An empty shoe box lay at his feet. His crumpled fedora was missing its feather, and his pinstriped shirt bore a thousand wrinkles. He never noticed. He was blind. But his ear was skillfully tuned to a mellow saxophone. His music told a story his heart knew all too well.

Dozens of people stood around, mesmerized by his magic. He volleyed between raspy singing and jazzy playing. We didn't know his lyrics, but it didn't matter. We loved the ragged old man in his raggedy old clothes anyway. His music hailed from another world, some unseen place beyond beignets and bystanders. He sang of dancing dandelions and purple skies, stolen kisses and sad good-byes.

Our two-hour shopping spree was over. We had to drive back to Picayune and get ready for church that night, but I felt compelled to chat with him when the time was right. I had to know more. How could he sing of such a beautiful place while living in such a dreary world?

His song ended. Spectators clapped and dropped money in his box. He removed the mouthpiece, wiped it on a rag, and mumbled something that struck me as a prayer.

"Excuse me, sir. May I ask you a question?" I said from eight feet away. I was holding a cup of coffee in one hand and a shopping bag in the other. He never responded. I raised my voice and tried again. "Sir, I really like your music. May I ask you a question?" No response.

A lady stepped from behind him and walked my way. "Myles can't hear out of his right ear," she said as she touched her ear, winked, and walked away. I chose not to make a scene, so I dropped a gift in his box and said, "Have a good day, sir." I was close enough to hear his mumble, "Thank ya, Jesus. O thank ya, thank ya, Jesus."

Myles didn't hear me, but I heard him loud and clear. We turned to walk to our car, and from a block away I heard the notes of his next song.

> *Amazing grace! How sweet the sound*
> *That saved a wretch like me!*
> (JOHN NEWTON)[1]

That was thirty years ago. I can't remember what I bought in the French Quarter that day, but I remember who I met. I met a blind man with a saxophone in his hand, a song in his heart, and a prayer on his lips.

If a half-deaf, blind man can sing a song in the bayou breeze, if Jesus Christ can sing a hymn the night before his execution (Mark 14:26), if Corrie ten Boom can sing a tune from a Nazi prison camp, if Paul and Silas can sing at midnight in a Philippian jail cell (Acts 16:25), then I can sing my song on the best of days or the worst of nights.

The Gospel according to Myles: never let your circumstances steal your song.

_____

> *I will bless the* LORD *at all times; His praise shall*
> *continually be in my mouth.*
> (PSALM 34:1)

SEVEN

Aching Achan

Achan stuck his head out of the tent door and looked around. The coast was clear. Neighbors had settled in for the night and all was quiet, except for the wild goat rustling in the grass on the hillside. He cupped his hands to his mouth and mimicked the croak of a swamp toad. His son heard the cue and dashed in the dark from the woodshed to the tent door.

"Did you bring the shovel and the satchels?"

"Yes, sir. No one saw me."

"Good boy."

The wife and daughter rolled up the rug in the center of the room, exposing the dirt floor. "Shh. Go keep a lookout," Achan said. Like an escapee tunneling out of prison, he dumped shovelfuls of dirt into the satchels. His kids sneaked the dirt behind the woodshed and sifted it among the shavings. Once the mini-grave was dug, Achan wiped his hands and took one more gander from the tent door. The whole camp of Israel slumbered and slept.

Then he brought his loot out in the open, 200 silver coins. His family grinned and gawked. "And look at this," Achan said as he curled a wedge of gold like a barbell. His son reached out. "No. No. Don't touch it. Just look." Then Achan held up a sleek Babylonian garment, embroidered with purple and bedecked with jewels.

"Ahh!" His wife's mouth fell wide open. "The Mantle of Shinar. Can I try it on?" Achan wrapped it around her shoulders and gave her a kiss. A single candle cast their criminal shadows across the grave that would hide the loot he pillaged from Jericho's plunder.

Achan spread the silver in the bottom of the hole, placed the gold bullion in the middle, and folded the garment over the top. After that, his wife tucked sheepskin over the hidden treasure and rolled the rug back in place. The dirty deed had been done. They crawled into bed and pretended nothing had happened. But for Achan, moonlight never felt so cold. Midnight never felt so dark.

29

Israel's next battle, against the tiny town of Ai, was met with devastating defeat. Joshua ripped his clothes in grief and fell on his face before the ark of the Lord. "But the LORD said to Joshua, 'Get up! Why are you lying on your face like this? Israel has sinned and broken my covenant!'" (Joshua 7:10-11 NLT).

The next day, Joshua began to ferret out the criminal, first by clan, then by family, and finally man by man. The cast die fell upon Achan. He stood before the elders, guilty as sin, still feeling that somehow he deserved the plunder of war. His wife stood proudly with him and stared at Joshua without batting an eye.

Soldiers marched to Achan's tent and returned with the stolen goods. "Then Joshua and all the Israelites took Achan, the silver, the robe, the bar of gold, his sons, daughters, cattle, donkeys, sheep, goats, tent, and everything he had, and they brought them to the valley of Achor. Then Joshua said to Achan, 'Why have you brought trouble on us? The LORD will now bring trouble on you'" (Joshua 7:24-25 NLT). Judgment was swift and severe.

Ever since that time, the Valley of Achor has been known as the Valley of Trouble. The sad commentary of Achan's demise leaves us with the somber reality of our own guilt. Have we sinned? Do we deserve judgment? Have we hidden our dirty deeds?

Yes, but I have good news. Through the prophet Hosea, the Lord said he would "transform the Valley of Trouble into a gateway of hope" (Hosea 2:15 NLT). Ultimately, the door of hope and the gateway to freedom is Jesus.

Without Christ in our life, Achan's fate is our future. But with Jesus in our life, the ache of sin is gone and the joy of forgiveness lives forever.

He gave his life to free us from every kind of sin.
(TITUS 2:14 NLT)

EIGHT

My Backyard Hero

I grew up in a time when superheroes wore capes and boots. The best of the bunch was faster than a speeding bullet and more powerful than a locomotive. But one day, when I was about seven years old, I found out not all heroes change clothes in phone booths. One hero changed clothes at my house in the bedroom down the hall. He didn't wear red boots, blue tights, or a prominent "S" on his chest. Instead, he wore blue jeans, a tee shirt, and tennis shoes. I'm talking about my older brother, Bobby—my backyard hero.

We were both at the neighbor's house playing on the swing set when I got injured. I pushed the empty glider away from me to see how high it would go. When it swung back toward me, the sharp corner of the seat ripped through my left forearm. It sliced through my flesh like wartime shrapnel. Blood gushed, I screamed, and a hero was born.

Without fear or trepidation, my brother picked me up, slung me over his shoulder, climbed a chain-link fence, sprinted down the back alley, toted me into our house, and laid me down at my father's feet.

Mom and Dad wrapped a cloth around my wound and rushed me to the local hospital. Doctors stopped the bleeding and sewed me back together again. I've borne the proof of my injury for more than fifty years. The permanent scar on my left arm is not an ugly reminder of a fateful day, it's a reminder of my brother's heroic deed.

When I see the scar, I see my brother's concern. When I feel the crevice, I feel my brother's love. What I remember most is not the pain, the blood, or the trauma. My greatest memory is riding on my brother's back. I remember him galloping through a gauntlet of danger, like a war horse in a war zone.

In my seven-year-old mind, it was battlefield heroism, a Medal of Honor run. It was one soldier saving the life of another. I remember thinking everything's going to be okay because my brother can go the distance. And I was right. I made it home because he made it home.

Did you know Jesus is your battlefield brother? "Jesus and the people he makes holy all belong to the same family. That is why he isn't ashamed to call them his brothers and sisters" (Hebrews 2:11 CEV). He's your brother-in-arms because he bares you up in his arms.

As your brother, Jesus is your most reliable friend. He's got your back. He won't let you face trouble alone. He will always come to your rescue. He knows when you're lying and doesn't hold back the truth. Jesus knows how to make you laugh; he knows what makes you cry. He knows your faults and failures and loves you just the same. He knows the worst of your past; he plans the best for your future. He's your hero because he's your brother.

Jesus's acts of heroism are too many to name. He touched a leper with his own hand when no one else would touch him with a ten-foot pole. He silenced the storm when his disciples were frightened. Jesus healed a blind man in Jericho, an invalid in Bethesda, and a demoniac in Gadara. He walked on water, walked up Calvary's hill, and walked out of the grave.

But the greatest thing your brother ever did was carry you on his back. He saw you in your pain, and he couldn't walk away. He lifted you up from your fallen state and bore you on his shoulder. He trudged a bloody trail and climbed a rugged cross. He bled in your place. He took your scars two thousand years ago, and he still has the marks to prove it today.

Why? Why would Jesus do such a thing?

Because that's what a good brother does. He carries you on his back to get you where you belong: in your father's house.

He isn't ashamed to call them his brothers and sisters.
(HEBREWS 2:11 CEV)

NINE

Strange Shamgar

I might look strange, but I'm glad my parents didn't name me Strange. Shamgar, one of the judges of Israel (Judges 3:31), was not so lucky. According to Ellicott's Commentary, Shamgar means "name of a stranger."[1] Did his dad look at him the day he was born, raise his eyebrows and say, "Wow, what a strange looking kid," and the nickname stuck? Was there something strange about his features, like a red nose on a reindeer? I don't think so.

Most likely his name means stranger in the context of a foreigner, especially considering his father's name, Anath, is not a Jewish name. My best guess is he was born into a strange family (Jewish mother, non-Jewish father), under strange circumstances, in a strange land, during a strange time. So they named him Strange as a perpetual reminder of his fanciful origin.

His name is found in only two verses in the Bible (Judges 3:31, Judges 5:6), but don't let that fool you into thinking he wasn't important. What did he do? He slew six hundred Philistines with a farming instrument known as an ox goad. His courageous act of faith rescued his family and delivered his nation.

Here's Shamgar's story in a nutshell. A strange boy, born into a strange family during strange times, used a strange weapon under strange circumstances to deliver a people estranged from God. Now that's strange. But it sounds exactly like something God would do.

Do you live in strange times? Have you seen strange events in the news lately? Do you feel like a stranger at work, at school, or in your own house? Do you have a strange family? If so, you qualify as a modern-day Shamgar. God can use you to make a big difference in the lives of people all around you. How? Just watch Shamgar battle the Philistines. He'll show you.

You remember the Philistines, don't you? They were the bad boys from the badlands. Their Mount Rushmore would include some well-known faces: a bully named Goliath and a beauty named

Delilah. The Philistines are the Bible's version of Nordic Vikings. They were a seafaring people with a bloodthirsty appetite for war. Their combat style was shock and awe.

Take a ringside seat. I'll introduce the fighters. In the red corner are the war-hardened Philistines. They hail under the banner of five warlords from the Mediterranean coast. They are battle scarred and brutal. The Philistines are the only enemy of Israel crazy enough to steal the Ark of the Covenant, gouge out the eyes of Samson, and boast a champion nine feet six inches tall. They are a cut-throat gang with a street-thug mentality "straight outta Compton."

In the blue corner is a stranger to these parts, an inexperienced, unknown farmer named Shamgar. He's the guy with an ox goad in his hand and sweat on his brow.

Who's your money on, the Philistine prizefighters or the Israelite farmer with a pool stick in his hand and manure on his sandals? Mine is on Shamgar, not because of the weapon in his hand but because of the coach in his corner. Alpha and Omega has never lost a fight. He razed the impregnable walls of Jericho. He routed the entrenched demons in Gadara. He raised the entombed dead in Bethany. He's not intimidated by six hundred Philistines. He has legions of angels at his disposal.

This same God is in your corner. Are you fighting a different brand of Philistines? Not spear-wielding Goliaths or hip-swinging Delilahs, but an enemy just as deadly: cancer, Covid, and clogged arteries. Your struggle is with an irritating coworker, an irresponsible child, or an irate husband. Are the odds stacked against you six hundred to one? Don't panic. The One in your corner is undefeated. Even if you get knocked down, you'll never be counted out.

When Shamgar's battle against the Philistines was over, he was the only guy left standing. He earned six hundred notches in his belt in a single day. Don't let that surprise you. Peter saw three thousand converts after a single sermon, and Jesus can wash away a million sins with a single drop of blood.

Hey stranger, I have good news. When others rail against you, God rallies for you.

If God is for us, who can be against us?
(ROMANS 8:31)

TEN

Eli the Priest

The old man laid still in the quiet of the night. His lamp went out and a trail of smoke curled through the air and draped over him in a thick fog. He coughed, pulled the cover over his shoulder, and tucked it under his beard. The night was cold. His relationship with God was colder. Eli was a shadow of his former self. His strength was gone. His heart was weak. His eyes were nearly blind. He hadn't heard the voice of God in a long time.

As priest, he used to serve the altar. As high priest, he used to influence the nation. He was supposed to be the guardian of the Tabernacle, but under his watch, sacrilege had replaced the sacred. Immorality was the new reality. His two sons, Hophni and Phinehas, lived on the holy grounds, but they didn't live holy lives. Their sordid behavior and Eli's tolerance of it caused Yahweh to withhold his revelation (1 Samuel 3:1). God refused to speak because they refused to listen.

A thick curtain separated the Holy Place from their sleeping quarters. Veiled in silence, the seven-stemmed menorah glowed red throughout the chilly night. Nearby, the Ark of the Covenant sat beneath the wings of cherubs and the single eye of God watched from the mercy seat.

When Eli started snoring, God started talking. He whispered a single word: "Samuel." The voice carried down the hallway, passed the old man's chamber, and reached into the room of his understudy.

The young boy sat up in bed. "Yes?" He threw the covers off and ran to Eli's room. "Did you call me?"

"No, I didn't call you. Go back to sleep."

God watched from the Holy Place and never blinked. As soon as Eli drifted off, God whispered again, "Samuel."

The boy's feet hit the floor. He ran to Eli's bedside. "Yes? I heard you call my name."

"No. You must be dreaming. Go lie down."

The third time, Eli fell asleep. The third time, God whispered, "Samuel."

He ran to Eli's room yet again. "I heard you call me. I'm sure of it."

Eli realized what was going on. "Samuel, it's not my voice you heard. It's the voice of Yahweh. When he calls again, don't run to me; run to him."

By this time, the old man was wide awake. He relit his lamp and paced the floor, meditating on his mistakes. He had falsely accused Hannah of drunkenness. His sons had stolen sacrificial meat from the house of God, and he winked it off. They had also prostituted women in the sanctuary; he shrugged a shoulder. The voice of prophecy had been stifled under his administration, and he had learned to live without it.

Eli looked down the hallway and saw a divine glow emitting from Samuel's room. He gasped and laid his hand over his mouth. He tiptoed toward Samuel's room and tried to eavesdrop on the Eternal, but he heard nothing. So he returned to his room and trembled until morning's light. Judgment was coming. He felt it in his bones.

That night God chose to speak to a young boy rather than an old man, not because of his age, but because of his tender heart. Samuel was yielded and submissive, while Eli was resistant and self-serving. Both lived in God's house, but only one lived for God's glory. Young Samuel went to sleep as a protege. He woke up, a prophet.

In the morning, Eli said, "What *is* the word that *the* LORD spoke to you? Please do not hide *it* from me" (1 Samuel 3:17).

It was a word of rebuke, a word of judgment, and Samuel didn't sugarcoat it. He told it just like it was, holding nothing back. Within a few days, Eli died a horrible death. What happened to the young prophet? "As Samuel grew up, the LORD was with him, and everything Samuel said proved to be reliable" (1 Samuel 3:19 NLT).

Lesson learned: Rejecting God's ways leads to judgment, but walking in God's ways leads to success.

For the wages of sin is death, but the gift of God is eternal
life in Christ Jesus our Lord.
(ROMANS 6:23)

ELEVEN

A Boy Named Jeremy

I stood at the chilly graveside, wool hat in hand, and watched a grieving mother wrestle with unanswered questions. Jeremy was only seventeen, too young to die.

I wasn't attending the funeral in an official capacity. I was only there to support my pastor friend since I was in town for a few days. I bowed my head for prayer and listened to the sobs of those who loved him, all the while wishing I had known him better.

My only memory of the deceased was a brief encounter the year before. They rolled Jeremy down the church aisle in his wheelchair. I noticed right away he was a victim of cerebral palsy. His legs were thin and distorted, his head was supported by a neck brace, and his arms were twisted across his body. But it was his smile that was unmistakable. He was the happiest guy in church.

He mumbled something. I nodded politely and said, "I'm glad you're here today." He mumbled again. It was the same three syllables as before, but I didn't have a clue what he said. It sounded like "Gold on dew" in a slurred sort of way.

Drool dripped onto the bib that covered his clothes. He raised his voice and tried again, "Gold on dew." His mother turned around just in time to translate. "Yes, Jeremy, God is good."

"God is good," I said, still looking in his eyes.

He celebrated with wild enthusiasm. If he could have clapped his hands and danced a jig, he would have. The wheelchair shook with applause as his smile grew wider. I got the message: God is good, and he got the blessing of being understood.

On the day of the funeral, the graveside tent couldn't cover the whole family. Droves of friends from far and wide showed up to remember the life of this teenage marvel. I stood on the outskirts of the crowd, shivering in the brisk January breeze.

"We are going to let Jeremy preach his own funeral," the pastor said. He held up a recorder and pushed the play button. I heard the same grunt I'd heard the year before, "Gold on dew." Right on cue the entire crowd shouted, "God is good."

I blinked to keep from crying. How dare I complain about anything in life. If a wheelchair-bound boy can utter "God is good" with slurred speech and crossed eyes, certainly I can push through my doubts and disappointments and shout the same thing.

"Now Jeremy's going to choose the Scripture we read today," the pastor said. He pushed play on the recorder again and we heard, "Tu-tee." The pastor asked the mother to confirm.

"Twenty-three, she said. His favorite verse is Psalm 23,"

One of Jeremy's classmates stood up and read, "The LORD *is* my shepherd; I shall not want. He makes me . . ."

My handkerchief couldn't hold my tears. I wept as I pondered the fact that a boy who couldn't walk on his own two feet had learned to "walk through the valley of the shadow of death" and "fear no evil." Although he couldn't feed himself, he trusted the God who prepares "a table before me in the presence of my enemies." With drool dripping down his chin, Jeremy could still proclaim, "My cup runs over" with the blessings from the Lord.

"There's one other verse we are going to read today," the pastor said. On the recorder we heard Jeremy mumble, "Nan jun," with his best linguistic effort.

"That's ninety-one. Psalm 91." Jeremy's brother sniffled his way through that beloved chapter. I only heard the first part because my mind drifted to my own experience with that same Psalm—the time when my wife and I sat in front of a neurologist in the conference room at MCV. "He who dwells in the secret place of the Most High shall abide under the shadow of the Almighty" (Psalm 91:1).

After the funeral, I understood God's goodness better. When an invalid boy's mumbles sound like "Gold on dew. Tu-tee. Nan jun," God understands and hears something totally different. Beyond bibs and wheelchairs, in spite of twisted limbs and crossed eyes, in lieu of grunts and mumbles, the Lord hears the deep cry of the soul, "God is good. He is my shepherd and my hiding place."

I will say of the LORD, "He is my refuge and my fortress;
my God, in Him I will trust."
(PSALM 91:2)

TWELVE

The Shunamite

Elisha snuffed out the candle in the upstairs room and laid down on the bed under an open window. He closed his eyes and listened to the cadence of a thousand crickets on a midsummer night in the tiny town of Shunem.

The contentment he felt in his heart was like that of a father when his children are safe and sound, tucked in tight, and kissed goodnight. His deep sigh was more than relief from the heat of the day or the rise and fall and turns and twists of his arduous trip from Carmel. He was home again, in a manner of speaking, although a two-day trek from his personal residence.

His frequent stops in Shunem had rewarded him with the friendship of a well-to-do couple, who welcomed him into their home any time he needed a place to stay. And of all the places he traveled, far and wide, only Shunem felt like home away from home.

Gehazi, his servant, lay in the corner on a mat and rubbed his aching belly. Why go home at all, with roasted lamb piled high on the dinner table and a basket of grapes in the guest room? "Ah! This is the life," he said after a hearty belch. Both of them slept the night away, beneath a moonlit sky with just enough breeze to snuggle under the finest sheepskin in all the land.

They awoke in the morning to the smell of breakfast. Elisha stepped into his sandals and splashed water in his face. Gehazi slipped into a robe and combed through his wiry hair with one hand. "Big-time breakfast, here I come," he said as he bolted for the door.

"Wait." Elisha grabbed his friend by the shoulder and squeezed hard enough to prove he was serious. "The Shunamite and her husband have lavished us with all this care. Every luxury of theirs has become ours. We shouldn't eat another bite until we repay kindness for kindness."

Gehazi's eyes widened. "What do you have in mind?"

"Go downstairs and bring her back up here. Let nothing restrain you, poached eggs nor proper etiquette."

Elisha sat on the bed and waited for their return. After a subtle knock, Gehazi stuck his neck around the door. "Master, she's at the top of the stairs but refuses to come closer; her husband's not home."

Elisha said, "Tell her, 'We appreciate the kind concern you have shown us. What can we do for you? Can we put in a good word for you to the king or to the commander of the army?'" (2 Kings 4:13 NLT).

Gehazi stepped outside and returned a moment later. "Sir, she said she doesn't need any favors from the king, the commander, or the prophet."

Elisha got up and walked to the window in silence. A hint of rain was in the air as clouds gathered over the Jezreel Valley. "As certain as summer rain brings fall harvest, we will not leave this town until—"

"Master," Gehazi interrupted, "I know the one thing she wants more than anything. What is prosperity without posterity? She has a husband, but she has no son."

Elisha turned with a snap and pointed a finger. "Call her at once."

As she reached the top of the steps, this time Elisha broke protocol and addressed her face to face. "Next year at this time you will be holding a son in your arms!" (2 Kings 4:16 NLT).

She backpedaled. She blushed. She bowed. "Don't say that, man of God. My hopes have been crushed too many times. Why break my heart again?"

Nine months later, when purple iris dotted the foothills of Moreh and spring wildflowers ran like wild gazelles through the valley, Elisha and Gehazi stopped by Shunem's newest nursery to visit a mother whose dream had come true, a lady who found out firsthand that God's faithfulness exceeds our kindness.

God will reward each of us for what we have done.
(ROMANS 2:6 CEV)

THIRTEEN

Jeremiah the Prophet

Jeremiah's body was twisted like a pretzel. His back ached, his neck cramped, and his wrists burned like fire. The contraption he was fastened to was designed to inflict maximum pain. There were five clasps in all; two confined his legs, two restrained his hands, and one squeezed tightly around his neck. This tangle was more than most people could bear, even for a few minutes. Yet the prophet hung suspended all night in its vicious grip. He couldn't sleep a wink. Minutes crept like hours. Every inhale, he moaned. Every exhale, he groaned. And a priest named Pashhur was responsible for it all.

"When the priest Pashhur . . . heard Jeremiah prophesying these things, he had Jeremiah the prophet beaten and put in the stocks at the Upper Gate" (Jeremiah 20:1-2 NIV).

While all of Jerusalem slept the night away, Jeremiah hung under the stars and tried to relieve the pain. He winced. He wept. He wiggled. Nothing helped.

On the darkest night of his life, he was not alone. God was with him, pouring out mercy and pouring in grace. At his weakest moment, I believe Jeremiah meditated on Psalm 31. Why?

Take note of what Jeremiah said when the sun came up. "Then on the next day, when Pashhur released Jeremiah from the stocks, Jeremiah said to him, 'Pashhur is not the name the Lord has called you, but rather Magor-missabib'" (Jeremiah 20:3 NASB).

The Hebrew phrase *Magor-missabib* means "terror on every side"[1] and is a direct quote from Psalm 31. "For I hear many whispering, 'Terror on every side!'" (Psalm 31:13 NIV).

Perhaps Jeremiah held on during the night by identifying with the psalmist. David had been surrounded by terror in his affliction. And in order to survive, he meditated on God's goodness and sang songs in the night. Jeremiah, the weeping prophet, followed David's

41

example. All throughout that painful night, in between his moans and groans, he whispered God's promises and trusted God's faithfulness.

Look what happened. God turned the tables. In the days that followed, it was not Jeremiah but Pashhur who was surrounded by terror. The New Testament teaches us that God will not be mocked. "Whatever a man sows, that he will also reap" (Galatians 6:7).

I marvel that Jeremiah thought on Psalm 31 while hanging in the stocks, because years later Jesus quoted the same Psalm while hanging on the Cross. "Into Your hand I commit my spirit" (Psalm 31:5).

Separated by more than six hundred years, Jeremiah and Jesus both endured their darkest hour meditating on the same Psalm. It sustained them. It will sustain you too.

Perhaps you struggle today. Your emotions are twisted. Your circumstances are painful. Your relationships are strained. Hang in there like Jeremiah did, like Jesus did. Meditate on God's promises.

In You, O LORD, I put my trust;
Let me never be ashamed;
Deliver me in Your righteousness.
Bow down Your ear to me,
Deliver me speedily;
Be my rock of refuge,
A fortress of defense to save me.
(PSALM 31:1-2)

FOURTEEN

Uncle Archie

I called him Uncle Archie, although he wasn't my uncle. He was a tobacco farmer in eastern North Carolina back when June bugs plagued the day and lightning bugs placated the night. He and his wife lived in an old farmhouse beside a tall barn in the middle of a broad field. The house boasted a large front porch, shaded by pecan trees and guarded by old hound dogs.

Uncle Archie would've never won a beauty contest, unless you were looking for big hearts; then he might come in first place. His nose was crooked, his hair was uncombed, and his jaw was crammed full of snuff. Juice leaked from the corners of his mouth and dripped onto his shirt, already soaked with a day's worth of sweat.

The highlights of the house, from my childhood memories, were homemade biscuits on the lazy Susan and spittoon buckets in the living room. Spinning table tops at dinner and spitting in the house at random were treats I never enjoyed living in Virginia.

Early one morning, while staying at Uncle Archie's house, I got my first taste of slopping the hogs. If you've never had the "heebie jeebies," you've never slopped hogs at sunrise on an empty stomach. Every "heebie" in me tried to "jeebie." That was the day I decided not to be a farmer. Cropping tobacco and slopping hogs is at the bottom of my wish list, right along with hugging porcupines and kissing skunks.

That's what shocks me about the Prodigal Son in Luke 15. While slopping the hogs, I held my nose, but he licked his lips. I reached for the barf bag. He reached for a fork and spoon. I said yuk. He said yum. What is it with this guy? How hungry do you have to be to drool over pig slop?

"He persuaded a local farmer to hire him, and the man sent him into his fields to feed the pigs. The young man became so hungry that even the pods he was feeding the pigs looked good to him" (Luke 15:15-16 NLT).

You know you are living too far from the Father's house when things that are bad for you start looking good to you. When sin becomes appetizing, when temptation becomes tantalizing, that's your sign; you're knee deep in the pig pen and it's time for a change—a change of scenery, a change of direction, and a change of heart.

"When he finally came to his senses, he said to himself, 'At home even the hired servants have food enough to spare, and here I am dying of hunger! I will go home to my father'" (Luke 15:17-18 NLT).

When the boy finally went back home, his father threw a party. They killed the fattest calf, invited neighbors to the party, and played music late into the night. If you could have interviewed the boy the next day, he would have told you, "There's no place like home."

So what are you waiting for? Your first step away from the pig pen is your first step toward your Father's arms. The dinner bell is ringing. The door is open. What will it be, slop in a trough or supper with your Father? The choice is yours.

While he was still a long way off,
his father saw him coming.
(LUKE 15:20 NLT)

FIFTEEN

The Speechless Priest

The morning sun peeked over the horizon and woke up the sleepy hamlet of Ein Karem, a charming little town tucked between the folds of the southern hills of Judea. Most villagers rolled over in their beds for forty more winks, but not Zechariah. He was already on his feet. How could he sleep? He'd waited six long months for this day to come. As a priest in the course of Abijah, it was his duty to serve God in the Temple for the next seven days, and it would be half a year before he'd get to do it again.

He packed his leather satchel and slung it over his donkey, then walked back to the house to kiss his wife goodbye. Elizabeth was just as excited as he. She loved hearing stories about the City of David once her husband returned from sacred service. Teasing, he rubbed his nose against hers.

"Behave yourself, old man," she winked.

"Goodbye, Dear," he said. "I'll see you in a few days. Now help me get on this donkey. I'm not as spry as I used to be."

She had no way of knowing those would be the last words she'd hear him say for the next ten months. In a week's time he'd be as dumb as a donkey, spooked into silence by an angel.

When he arrived in Jerusalem, olive trees hung wet with morning dew and spring flowers dotted the valley below. Dozens of priests arrived at the same time, each one chomping at the bit to serve in the Temple for the next seven days, seven glorious days.

The next morning they all stood in a circle waiting for the High Priest to divvy up their duties. Assignments were determined by Urim and Thummim (an ancient way of rolling dice). Each man hoped it fell his turn to offer incense on the golden altar.

And so it happened, on that chilly morning, that the Urim fell upon Zechariah, and the old dream of an old man became a new hope for the new Messiah.

Zechariah cradled a scoop of incense in a handheld shovel and stepped into the holy sanctum. He smelled fresh bread on the table to his right. He saw flames of the menorah dancing in bowls on his left. The old priest took cautious steps forward until he felt the heat of burning coals on his ashen face.

He sprinkled powdered incense on the golden lid and was instantly shrouded in a cloud of smoke. The heady perfume buckled his knees. His hands shook. His eyes watered. His heart raced. He tried to pray, but only whispers escaped his trembling lips. Then he gasped. In the hallowed haze before him stood a mighty angel.

"Do not be afraid, Zechariah; your prayer has been heard. Your wife Elizabeth will bear you a son" (Luke 1:13 NIV). Zechariah couldn't believe it, so Gabriel spoke again, "You will be silent and not able to speak . . . because you did not believe my words" (Luke 1:20 NIV).

A week later, Zechariah rode back to Ein Karem, as silent as the day was long. His communication was limited to signs by hand and scribbles on parchment. In the silence of his home, the spoken word of the Lord came to pass. An old man and an old woman conceived a baby, and not just any baby; he would be known as the "voice of one calling" (Mark 1:3 NIV). How ironic. The voiceless priest fathered the voice of a prophet.

On the eighth day, when John was circumcised, heaven released his father's tongue. For the first time in nearly a year, Zechariah was free to speak. A song replaced his silence. A hallelujah replaced his hush. It was a sign of what was to come. "Praise be to the Lord, the God of Israel, because he has come to his people and redeemed them" (Luke 1:68 NIV).

So it was, Zechariah's first words announced the coming Redeemer. And like father, like son, John announced, "the Lamb of God . . . takes away the sin of the world" (John 1:29 NIV). Silence rules no more. Good News rings clear.

Our role today is still the same. Whether in the wilderness or Walmart, in Jerusalem or Jersey Mike's, in Samaria or Starbucks, we are to share the good news, "Messiah has come, and his name is Jesus."

Don't be afraid! Speak out!
(ACTS 18:9 NLT)

SIXTEEN

Mrs. Mable

A routine hospital visit turned into a glimpse of heaven. Mrs. Mable was recovering from multiple surgeries after her car accident, but her out-of-body experience came when she died in the ambulance.

"Some people don't believe in angels," she said, "but I do. I saw them when I wrecked my car."

"Oh, I believe in angels," I said. "I saw two of them in my bedroom when I was a teenager. But I don't tell people, because they'd think I'm crazy."

Mable's eyes lit up. "Let me tell you about my angels. This is going to sound crazy, but my soul came out of my body seconds before the accident happened. Two angels pulled me out of the car before it slammed into the bridge. I watched the accident happen from twenty feet in the air, so I never felt pain when my car wrecked."

"Wow! I never heard of such a thing."

"I know. I think God knew it was going to happen, so he spared me all the trouble and took me a split second early."

"What happened after that?"

"Well, I always thought angels were feminine, but these angels looked like big men. They were tall and muscular with blonde hair and transparent eyes.

"And they had big, beautiful, powerful wings. When the angels flew, you could hear a whoosh sound. They escorted me up through a tunnel of light, where there are two things I distinctly remember: the tunnel was full of beautiful colors, and I could hear music playing."

"What do you mean exactly?"

"How many colors come in a big box of crayons, sixty-four?"

"Umm, I'm not sure."

"Well, in that tunnel of light, it was more like a thousand. There are colors in heaven we don't have on earth. It was spectacular. And the music . . . it sounded like millions of voices, millions of beautiful voices."

"What were they singing?"

"They were all singing different songs."

"What? At the same time?"

"Yes, at the same time, but it blended together like one choir. I couldn't see who was singing, but it sounded like all of heaven. Just imagine if rainbows could sing, what would it sound like? Now fill the sky with millions of rainbows, each one singing a different song, and that is what heaven sounds like."

"Wow, I'd love to hear that."

"When I came out of that tunnel, I was standing in a big green field. I felt young and energetic, like I was a kid again. I didn't have a pain in the world. My arthritis was gone. Carpal tunnel was gone. Fibromyalgia was gone. Everything was gone."

I laughed. "When you came out of that tunnel, you were a brand-new person, huh?"

"Yes, I was," she laughed. "The angels left me at that point, but I didn't feel alone. There is a voice, a presence, an all-seeing eye that is with you in heaven. You're never alone. Now, at the end of that grassy field, I saw a golden city. The walls were tall and glistening, and there was a halo of glory that covered the whole place. And the big gate at the front was wide open. You should have seen the number of souls going in, hundreds and thousands."

"Tell me about them."

"They were Christians who had died on earth. I'm telling you, they are going in by the thousands every day. I was in line to go in next. I got close enough to see inside the gate. There's a river that flows right through the middle of that place, with beautiful trees on both sides. And just before I stepped through that gate, the doctors brought me back to life in the ambulance. I kind of wish they had left me alone."

"But then I would have never heard your story, Mable. So I'm glad you're still with us."

The city had no need of the sun or of the moon to shine in
it, for the glory of God illuminated it.
(REVELATION 21:23)

SEVENTEEN

The Withered Hand

Come with me to Capernaum's synagogue, and watch Jesus do what only he can do.

See the guy in the corner? The one trying to hide in the crowd? His hand is in his pocket for a reason. It's withered and he's ashamed. He hopes to blend in with the crowd, to sneak into the synagogue and sit in the corner, to nod an amen and get out before the hand-shaking starts.

He's a worshipper but wounded. He's a believer but burdened. He's a member but mangled. So he sits quietly and doesn't make any waves, especially with that withered hand of his.

Sounds like some of us, doesn't it? We glance around the synagogue and think everyone else looks great. Their shoes are fashionable, their waistlines are thin, and their nails are manicured. Then we take a look at ourselves. Humph! We are pigeon-toed, bow-legged, pot-bellied, thick-necked, freckle-faced, and beady-eyed. We're messed up from the feet up, stared down from the head down. But here's the good news—we've been handpicked by the Promise Keeper, and he has a knack for doing wonderful things for wounded people.

"Step forward" (Mark 3:3).

Those were the last two words he wanted to hear. He didn't want center stage, he wanted the back row. He'd rather crawl out on his hands and knees than stand up there in front of all those people. Everyone in agreement raise your withered right hand and say amen.

Withered is such an ugly word. It describes crusty old leaves and shriveled up peas. Withered means the life has been sucked out, the beauty has faded, and the doldrums have set in. Relationships wither after a while, so do careers and plans, hopes and dreams.

Take a second look around the synagogue. See Adam? He's full of shame. Look at Samson. He's blind. And Jonah? He's bleached.

49

Rahab is soiled. Peter is prejudice. Thomas is doubtful. Judas is a thief. Demas is a wimp. And John Mark is a scaredy-cat. You're not the only one dealing with a problem. We're all in the same boat (err, all on the same pew.)

"Stretch out your hand" (Mark 3:5).

Here? Now? In front of all these people? These fault finders, back stabbers, and finger pointers?

What do you think motivated the man with a withered hand to stand in front of a crowd and expose his withered hand? It was the voice of Jesus, tender yet confident, persuasive yet patient. Something in the voice of Jesus touched something in the man's heart, and he decided to do what he thought he'd never do.

"He stretched *it* out, and his hand was restored as whole as the other" (Mark 3:5).

Jesus's goal was not to embarrass. It never is. His goal was to restore: to restore health, respect, significance, and a sense of value. After he was healed, the man was ready to shake some hands, to lend a helping hand, and to volunteer with a raised hand, a hand that used to be withered, a hand restored by Jesus.

So when you hear the voice of Jesus, don't stay hidden in the corner. Answer his call. Yield to his voice. You'll leave with a smile on your face, a pep in your step, and a twinkle in your eye. More than that, you'll leave restored where you used to be withered.

"I will give you back your health
and heal your wounds," says the LORD.
(JEREMIAH 30:17 NLT)

EIGHTEEN

Daughter

Daughter is one of the prettiest words in the English language. Just look at it. Eight different letters and each one cascades in curls like Goldilocks of fairytales.

Say it out loud: "Daughter." It rolls off of your tongue like poetry. Handwritten, it resembles artwork. A masterpiece, in fact. No other word communicates such strong feelings of endearment.

There's nothing in the world quite like a daughter: soft skin, dimpled cheeks, and trusting eyes. The earth stops revolving when she lifts her little arms and says, "Daddy, hold me." He's wrapped around her finger. She's wrapped around his heart. That's just the way it is, and nothing will ever change it.

Jesus never married or fathered children, yet he knew the tender love and lasting bond associated with the word daughter. In the New Testament, Jesus addressed one woman as daughter. That's right, just one woman. And when Jesus called her daughter, it changed everything in her life. We don't know her name, but we do know her story (Mark 5:25-34).

Her body was frail. Her condition was incurable. What little hope she held onto dropped faster than her blood pressure. Doctor after doctor sent her away with no cure. There was no procedure they could do and no prescription they could write. Her pocketbook was empty, although her tear ducts were full. We find her in a back alley with her back against the wall. But she had one thing going for her. Jesus was in town and walking in her direction. Hope was only a few steps away. Mercy was within arm's reach.

You've been there, haven't you? The place where disappointments fall like rain and clouds of doubt hide the light of day. The back alley of despair is full of bitter pills and broken promises. For what it's worth, you're not alone.

The widow from Zarephath was down to her last bite of food

(1 Kings 17:12), Elijah felt like quitting under a juniper tree (1 Kings 19:4), and Martha grieved after losing her brother (John 11:21). It's called real life in the real world. The real question is, have you heard about Jesus?

Apparently, reports about Jesus circulate in desperate places like back alleys, rock bottom, and down in the dumps. When the woman heard about Jesus, she decided to reach through the crowd and touch his garment. She believed she would be healed. And it worked.

"He looked round about to see her that had done this thing. But the woman fearing and trembling, knowing what was done in her, came and fell down before him, and told him all the truth" (Mark 5:32-33 KJV).

There are many truths to glean from her story. But don't let this one go unnoticed: Everyone needs encouragement.

"He said to her, 'Daughter, your faith has made you well. Go in peace, and be healed of your affliction'" (Mark 5:34).

How beautiful. He could have used any of these terms: woman, hey you, patient, victim, sufferer. But no. He chose the best word of all: daughter.

Her body had been healed moments before, but Jesus wouldn't let her go until her broken heart was mended too. Jesus restored her dignity, recovered her honor, and repaired her hope—all with a single word: daughter.

His message was loud and clear. "You belong in my family and I'm not ashamed of you." Her tears flowed again, this time with joy.

Jesus is not ashamed to call them brothers and sisters.
(HEBREWS 2:11 NIV)

NINETEEN

Grandma

It had been awhile since I'd last seen her, and I wasn't sure she would recognize me. But it was something I had to do, a compulsion I couldn't shake.

I followed my GPS down an unfamiliar road to an uncomfortable place, whispering prayers along the way, mile after mile. When I pulled into the parking lot, I looked in the mirror and dried my eyes. The receptionist pointed down the corridor and gave me a room number. A frog was in my throat and a question in my mind, "What if she doesn't know me?"

When I entered the room, I saw a bed in every corner, each cradling a little old lady, grayed with age and wrinkled by time. I found the right woman and knelt down on the floor beside her bed. With my face only inches away from hers, I said, "Hi, Grandma. This is your grandson, Cliff."

She opened her eyes, as best she could, and gave me half a smile. Her speech was slurred due to multiple strokes, "Hey there. I'm glad you came to see me."

We talked about a lot of things, mostly her family and her future. "I want to go home," she said. I knew she wasn't talking about her home in High Point, North Carolina. She was talking about that celestial city "whose builder and maker is God" (Hebrews 11:10), the place where her husband rests and the place where her Savior reigns. "I don't know why the Lord won't take me home, unless it's for one reason."

"What reason is that, Grandma?"

"All I do is lay here in this bed and pray day and night. All of my children are saved but one, and I spend all my time praying for him to come to the Lord, because when I die, no one will pray for him like I do."

"You're right, Grandma. It would take an army of intercessors to pray like you do."

Half an hour later I was on my way home reminiscing about our time together and thanking God for a praying grandmother. That was the last time I saw her alive. Since then, her son surrendered his life to Jesus. Just like Grandma prayed—the family circle is unbroken.

I wonder what it will be like the next time I see her. We won't meet in a nursing home; I can tell you that. And it won't be in a funeral home or a cemetery. The next time we meet, it'll be "just inside the Eastern Gate over there" (Isaiah G. Martin).[1] There will be no more suffering. No more strokes, no more weeping, no more tears, no more pain, and no more sorrow. "For the former things have passed away" (Revelation 21:4).

What will it be like when I see Grandma in heaven? I don't know, but I can just imagine that I'll walk through those pearly gates and see her standing there in all her glory. Not half a smile this time but a full smile, full of love and laughter.

I'll say, "Hi, Grandma. This is your grandson, Cliff."

And she'll say, "Hey there. I'm glad you came to see me."

No eye has seen, no ear has heard,
and no mind has imagined
what God has prepared
for those who love him.
(1 CORINTHIANS 2:9 NLT)

TWENTY

Ground Force Commander

The ground force commander called for a meeting of his troops, including seventy new recruits who had just arrived. The briefing room was not a typical classroom with desks, chairs, and marker boards. It was a grassy hillside near Capernaum, down by the water's edge. The rising sun punched a hole through the fog, and a fishing boat, moored to the dock, bobbed and weaved in the shallows.

"Alright fellas, listen up." Jesus spoke with a calm authority. He knew they would win the day before it even started. He stood with his back to the lake. They sat in a semicircle in front of him.

"Many of you will see live-action combat for the first time today. It's a riot out there. I'm sending you out like sheep in the midst of wolves. The insurgents think they own the place. But make no mistake, today we will push deep into their territory and drive them out. They won't know what hit them. It will require blood, guts, and tears on your part, and I'll accept nothing less. Got it?"

"Copy that," said several soldiers. They sat cross-legged on the ground, not a rucksack among them. No M4 rifles. No belt-fed machine guns. Instead, they wore knee-length tunics and strap-on sandals. They didn't look the part, but it didn't matter. They had been chosen for the task.

"Any questions?"

"What are we going up against?" one soldier asked.

"'Principalities and powers, rulers of darkness, spiritual wickedness in high places' (Ephesians 6:12). Their leader is Satan, a high-level terrorist with evil intent. He is a thief, a murderer, and a deceiver. The battlefield is dangerous. The enemy is real. The consequences are eternal. I need your *A game*. No slackers."

The briefing was interrupted by the rumble of a diesel engine. It sounded like a mighty rushing wind. When the Humvee stopped, Ruach HaKodesh, a superior intelligence officer, stepped out and whispered to Jesus. Then he patrolled the perimeter until the briefing was over.

"We just got some new intel. There's a legion of demons in Gadara." He turned and pointed across the lake. "Also, a man with an unclean spirit has been spotted in Capernaum."

The soldiers looked spooked. Jesus never batted an eye. "Our mission is simple: seize, clear, defend, and heal."

"'Don't take any money with you, nor a traveler's bag, nor an extra pair of sandals. And don't stop to greet anyone on the road' (Luke 10:4 NLT). When you enter a city, declare that the kingdom of God has come."

One soldier raised his hand. "I heard our enemy was undefeated."

"Negative. I saw him hit the dirt like lightning from out of heaven. Trust me on this one—when he feels resistance, he tucks tail and runs. Besides, 'the weapons of our warfare are *not* carnal but mighty in God for pulling down strongholds' (2 Corinthians 10:4). We own the skies." He pointed up. Two Apache gunships (Michael and Gabriel) hovered overhead. "Our intel is up-to-the-minute. Sync your radio with mine to Spirit channel Ephesians 6:18. It's a secure frequency. The enemy can't crack it.

"Don't be a Lone Ranger out there. Pair up. Cover and move, just like I taught you. And watch your brother's six. Friendly fire will not be tolerated. The enemy is out there, not in here. And leave no one behind."

Another soldier raised his hand. "I have no weapon. What am I supposed to fight with?"

"This is a spiritual battle. You fight with spiritual weapons. Use the faith I gave you. Keep my promises at hand. Pray and fast. Trust and obey. Cover and move."

Jesus radioed Ruach. "Send in the big guns."

Three M1A2 Abrams tanks rolled up. The ground crawled. Sand danced. Rocks bounced. Each tank bore a separate insignia: The Word, The Blood, and The Name.

"You have all the firepower you'll ever need right here. Up on your feet. Win the day. It's *game over* for the enemy. It's *game on* for us. Let's roll."

This is the victory that has overcome the world—our faith.
(1 JOHN 5:4)

TWENTY-ONE

The Infamous Con Man

If you like San Diego, you'll like Jericho. Both are hot spots for cool people who love palm trees and warm weather. With the top down on your convertible, it's a lovely Sunday drive from Jerusalem to Jericho. Turn the radio up and put the pedal down. You'll arrive before you know it, lickety-split.

But if you're walking the ancient path of two thousand years ago, grab your best pair of Nikes, a bottle of water, and a straw hat. It's an all-day trek. Circle around the Mount of Olives, skirt past Bethany, then lean back on your heels and slow step the descent for the next fifteen miles. You'll need a hammock, a glass of lemonade, and a foot massage when you get there. No worries though, Jericho's amenities satisfy even the crankiest traveler.

That's why, in Bible times, wealthy people gravitated toward Jericho. It was far enough from Jerusalem to escape the politics, and close enough to the beach to get a suntan. Wherever you find palm trees and summer breeze, you'll find spendthrifts and money sharks. And in New Testament times, Jericho had such a money shark. He was a wee little man with a knack for tree climbing. The infamous con man was a double-crossing, shady-dealing, blackmailing cheat named Zacchaeus.

The locals loathed the money mongrel and his shakedown tactics. He was an IRS agent with an attitude. He had Rome's authority to take the bling out of your bank account and the shirt off of your back. Zacchaeus was the most despised, most despicable, and most detested man in the whole community. So when Jesus decided to spend the night in the city of palms and chose Zacchaeus's house for his hotel, it infuriated everyone who heard about it. "The Rabbi's gone rogue. He darkened the door of a devil."

The next morning when Jesus headed off to Jerusalem, Zacchaeus made his rounds, knocking on the neighbors' doors. Women hid their children. Men hid their wallets. To their shock and surprise, he wasn't taking money, he was giving it away.

"My ledger says I overcharged you a hundred denarii last year. Here's a refund of four hundred. Forgive me. It won't happen again." By day's end he had given away half of his wealth.

"Zacchaeus, what happened? You changed overnight."

"When others hated me, Jesus loved me. People called me names, but he called me by my name. They threw rocks at my house, but Jesus dined in my house. When others cursed me to death, he offered me life."

And that's how the smallest man in Jericho became the biggest man in town.

Come down, for today I must stay at your house.
(LUKE 19:5)

TWENTY-TWO

Old Man with a New Hope

The Temple was busier than usual. Merchants sold their wares, Pharisees chanted prayers, Levites carted wood, and priests offered sacrifices. Every corner bustled with activity.

A roar of voices mixed and mingled among the crowd that day: local Judeans, out-of-town Galileans, and distant Gentiles. There seemed no method to the madness. Dads, moms, boys, and girls scurried in every direction.

Yet, in all the hustle and bustle, one old man walked among them marching to the beat of a different drum; he was unflappable, unfazed, and unhindered.

His posture was stooped and his steps were slow, consistent with his elderly stature. I must admit, there was a certain glow on his face that made me think he knew his time on earth was over. And he was rather happy about it.

Some folks interpreted his mumble as evidence of senility, but I noticed a rhythm and cadence in his voice that resembled an ancient song of David. I think the old man was jolly on the inside, and his lips tried to keep pace with his spirit. Like a classic song on a vinyl record, the tune was there, but it skipped and stuttered a bit.

On this particular day, he moved through the crowd with ease, like he knew something that no one else did. His name is Simeon, a patriarchal name meaning "heard."[1] What had this old man heard? And where was he headed?

Rumor has it that he'd heard the voice of God. He claims he can't die until he sees the Messiah. Ever since God made him that promise, he has searched the Temple, day after night, never giving up the hope. And he's back again today, looking for the Promised One.

"So he came by the Spirit into the temple. And when the parents brought in the Child Jesus, to do for Him according to the custom of the law, he took Him up in his arms and blessed God and said: 'Lord, now You are letting Your servant depart in peace, According to Your word; For my eyes have seen Your salvation'" (Luke 2:27-30).

Oh, what a blessed day. Simeon not only saw the Messiah, he held him in his hands—not at arm's length, but in the crook of his elbow, cradled close to his heart.

That's where Jesus belongs, right? He belongs right here, not way over there. His rightful place is near the heart and in the heart.

Most people, on that day, saw Mary's baby, not God's son. They saw dimples, not divinity. Who would guess those tiny toes would walk on water? Who would know those chubby cheeks would feel the kiss of betrayal? Who would venture to believe that his tender coo could raise Lazarus from the dead? No one knew those tiny fingers holding Mary's pinky would one day hold Roman spikes. The infant was Jesus, God's son, our Savior.

The bundle of joy in Mary's arms is the source of your joy. The one she wrapped in swaddling clothes wraps you in his love. The holy child with twinkles in his eyes never takes his eyes off of you. And the one newly born two thousand years ago offers you new birth today.

Don't let him get lost in the crowd. Don't let the noise of our times muffle his voice. Don't get so caught up rubbing shoulders with the world that you can't detect his tender touch.

He is here among us, Immanuel. Find him. Hold him. Adore him.

For my eyes have seen Your salvation which You have
prepared before the face of all peoples.
(LUKE 2:30-31)

TWENTY-THREE

Captain Jack

The call of seagulls overhead and the toll of the bell at Saint Peter's reminded Captain Jack he was home again. He sat all alone in his cabin below deck. *Jenny Two* was moored at the same slip from whence she'd sailed three months ago. The jolly crew, relieved of their duties, scattered throughout the bustling port for some well-deserved celebration.

Jack sat at his desk with his captain's log open awaiting its final entry. He jotted the date January 17, 1991, then stared at the blank page until he was embarrassed. He couldn't remember the last leg of their journey. He laid his pen in the crack of the book and walked over to his shaving mirror. The note taped in the corner read: "Things to remember: My name is Jack. My wife is Jenny. My Savior is Jesus." As he whispered the words a second time, he heard familiar footsteps on the deck and grinned. Only Jenny wore high heels on the ship, and only on his first night home. He stared at the closed door and waited for her grand entrance. A gentle tap sounded at the door.

"Who is it?" he said.

"You'll have to open the door to find out," she said playfully.

"I already know. It's my beauty queen," he said.

"Strike one," she said. "I'm no beauty queen."

Jack walked to the door and spoke louder, "But your high heels gave it away; it can be none other than my Queen of Hearts." He yanked the door open, and she leaped into his arms.

"Right you are, my dear." She kissed him over and over to make up for the twelve weeks he'd been at sea. He spun her around and kicked the door closed behind him.

"And we're all alone," he giggled.

"And I have a gift for you," she said.

"Hmm. A gift? What's the occasion?" Jack snapped his pocket-knife open and slit the envelope.

The note read, "McCally's @ 7."

Jack was puzzled. "McCally's?"

"It's your favorite restaurant, sweetheart. That's where you asked me to marry you." She pushed back a tear and rubbed the worried wrinkle off of his forehead.

"But I have to finish my log first."

"I'll help you, dear. We don't have much time. Your retirement party is waiting."

She crossed out the year 1991 and in her prettiest handwriting wrote, "The honorable Captain Jack, having concluded thirty adventurous years at sea and traveled the world from bow to stern, retires with dignity on this seventeenth day of January 2021."

"Just sign here, Jack."

"So, I'm retiring, eh?" He closed the book for the last time and placed it on the shelf. She pulled his travel bag behind them and walked to the gangplank wondering if he would remember this moment. She'd already determined to make every day together as joyful and memorable as possible.

The two held hands on the brisk walk to McCally's, pausing just long enough on the bridge to greet a young couple pushing a baby carriage. "Don't ever forget these precious times," Jack said. "You'll be old and retired before you know it." They chuckled in disbelief, like senior days were centuries away.

The hostess at McCally's took their bags and coats, then led them to the reserved room in the back. As soon as they stepped inside, the jam-packed crowd erupted, "For he's a jolly good fellow, which nobody can deny."

"All of this is for you, Jack, because we love you." Jenny kissed him. Food and fun filled the night, with gifts galore and pats on the back, until long at last the party was over.

"Jenny. What happens if one day I forget all of this, and forget my friends? What if I forget you?"

"Sweetheart, don't you worry about that. When the day comes that you don't know who I am, I'll still know who you are and love you just the same."

Love never fails.
(1 CORINTHIANS 13:8)

TWENTY-FOUR

Martha and Mary

The noise of Jerusalem's marketplace stands in contrast to the silence of Bethany's neighborhood, and the Mount of Olives stands as a barrier between them. The commercial hub on the west never sleeps. The cozy hamlet on the east never wakes. A Sabbath-day walk connects the two, but they are worlds apart.

No wonder Jesus stopped in Bethany on his way to Jerusalem. It was an opportunity to catch his breath before running his race toward Calvary. His momentary reprieve was a familiar place, a home he longed for and a family he loved. Rejected by the town behind him and hated by the city in front of him, he found a few friends in Bethany who embraced him. We know them as Mary, Martha, and Lazarus.

The light in their window signaled a rest stop for his weary bones, and their welcome mat made the long journey worth every step. Their roof protected him from the nippy night air, but more than that, it sheltered him from the cold criticism of his enemies.

Jesus needed a little down time before being strung up on a cross, and no place was better suited for it than the home of his closest friends. Sad to say, one of his friends completely missed the moment. While Jesus had his eye on the cross, Martha focused on a pot of beans. He wanted fellowship, she thought he wanted food. She was too busy making sure the bread didn't burn in the kitchen to realize the Bread of Life was sitting in the living room.

I commend Martha for her work ethic, but I loathe Martha's lack of perception. She wasn't listening to the whisper of his heart. Her ear was tuned to the whistle of a tea pot. While she watched the timer on the oven, his time was running out. Martha didn't have a clue, but Mary did.

Mary saw the grime of Bethany's dusty road on his feet, so she washed it away. Mary perceived he needed a friend, so she sat close by. Mary sensed something was heavy on his heart, so she opened her heart. As Jesus talked, she listened.

But not Martha. The more agitated she got, the faster she beat the eggs. She was froth with anger. She stepped out of the hot kitchen, hot under the collar. Sweat dripped off her nose. Flour spotted her clothes. She patted her foot on the floor and slapped a wooden spoon in her hand. The vein in her neck was a signal she had venom in her tongue.

"Lord, don't you care that my sister has left me to do the work by myself? Tell her to help me!" (Luke 10:40 NIV).

Martha thought Mary was wrong for doing nothing and Jesus was wrong for letting her get away with it.

Jesus raised his eyes, but not his voice. "Martha, Martha, you are worried and troubled about many things" (Luke 10:41).

Ahh! Now the truth comes to light. Martha was upset about a lot of things, not just dinner. She was perturbed about life. She didn't sleep well last night. The migraine lingered. Arthritis acted up. Metabolism ran low. Dishes filled the sink. Laundry flooded the basket. Money was running out. And she felt like running away.

All she really needed was right in front of her. A few minutes with the Eternal would have solved her temporary problems. Waiting on the Lord would have renewed her strength (Isaiah 40:31). Then she could have whistled while she worked and hummed a merry tune.

God forgive us for getting so caught up with life that we fail to spend time with the *Giver of Life*.

Give all your worries and cares to God,
for he cares about you.
(1 PETER 5:7 NLT)

TWENTY-FIVE

The Adulteress Woman

They caught her in the act, then they used her as bait. You know her story. The whole world knows. She is the adulteress woman in the city of Jerusalem who was caught *in flagrante delicto*. That's Latin for "in blazing offense."[1] These days we'd simply say she got caught red handed. No matter how you say it, she's guilty as sin.

We don't know her name. She's glad we don't. Not only was she exposed half naked in full view of the Temple crowd, but her shameful acts have been published all over the world.

She was victimized thrice: first by a pretend lover, second by hypocritical Pharisees, and third by folks today who look down their long noses with holier-than-thou accusations.

We know how she felt because we feel the same way—used and abused, stepped on and walked over, chewed up and spit out. The same standard-bearers and rule-book thumpers that lived back then roam the earth today.

"Teacher, this woman was caught in adultery, in the very act. Now Moses, in the law, commanded us that such should be stoned" (John 8:4-5).

She went from facing shame in the mirror to facing the death penalty at the Temple. She was yanked from the arms of Romeo and thrown down at the feet of the Rabbi so fast she didn't have time to put her clothes on or turn the red light off. That's what happens when rude men with cruel intentions care more about themselves than they do you.

Listen to the Pharisees. "'But what do You say?' . . . testing Him, that they might have *something* of which to accuse Him" (John 8:5-6).

Here's the clincher. The Pharisees were out to catch the big tuna, so they snagged a red herring first. This is the old bait and switch routine. She was guilty of adultery, but that wasn't the point. Her kind can be found a dime a dozen. The real target was the Teacher from Galilee, the rogue Rabbi who upset their apple cart. He had claimed to be the Son of God and was a direct threat to their "holy" society. The adulteress woman was merely a pawn in their hand. The Messiah was the king they wanted to checkmate.

"But Jesus stooped down and wrote on the ground with *His* finger, as though He did not hear" (John 8:6).

I love this part of the story. We have a court of law in session. The adulteress is on trial. "Raise your right hand. Do you solemnly swear to tell the truth, the whole truth, and nothing but the truth, so help you God?"

The God who was going to help her had knelt down beside her. He was her defense attorney. He had no legal pad, no Exhibit A, and no fancy fountain pen—just a finger in the dirt.

The prosecutors shouted accusations against her. But the defense attorney squatted in silence. The Pharisees held rocks in their hands, ready for an execution. Jesus held his peace, ready for an acquittal.

What a difference between the way people see us and the way Jesus sees us. They see our past. He sees our future.

"So when they continued asking Him, He raised Himself up and said to them, 'He who is without sin among you, let him throw a stone at her'" (John 8:7).

At first, you could hear a pin drop. Then you could hear rocks drop. One by one, they turned and walked away.

"Woman, where are those accusers of yours? Has no one condemned you?" (John 8:10).

She looked up for the first time since she'd been thrown down. "No one, Lord."

"Neither do I condemn you; go, and sin no more" (John 8:11).

Have sweeter words ever been spoken? The Innocent looked into the eyes of the guilty and withheld judgment. He knew her faults and failures, her sins and transgressions. But he offered her a way out. He opened the door of mercy and she stepped into freedom.

In the twelve verses that tell her story (John 8:1-12), she only said three words: "No one, Lord." It was her last word that was her saving grace.

Whoever calls on the name of the LORD shall be saved.
(ROMANS 10:13)

TWENTY-SIX

Mama's Boy

I whispered a prayer before stepping into the seedy joint. When the door closed behind me, I knew I'd made a mistake. Thick smoke filled the place, and every breath set my lungs on fire. Subwoofers pulsed, bottles rattled, and drunkards gyrated to honkytonk.

"Wanna beer?" a blonde waitress shouted above the music.

"No." I coughed. "I'm looking for a friend."

"It's your lucky day." She winked.

"No, his name is . . ." She spun around and disappeared into the crowd. I took a picture out of my pocket to jog my memory: dark hair, goatee, early thirties, and a tattoo on his neck. Jimmy should've been easy to spot, but half of the guys in there fit that description. His mother said he'd be there. I finally found him sitting at a high top, scrolling through his phone.

"Jimmy?"

He looked up, surprised. "Maybe. Maybe not."

"Your mother sent me," I said as I showed him the picture.

He laughed. "You're either a cop or a preacher."

"Guilty as charged. I'm a preacher."

He took a swig of his drink. "So, you're here to save me."

"Your mother's concerned about you."

"Then why'd she kick me out of the house? Don't believe everything that woman says. She lies like a dog."

"She didn't lie this time. She said you'd be here. Mind if I sit?"

"It's a free country."

"What are you looking for in a place like this?"

"Peace, from people like you . . . and Mama."

"Hmm. Sounds like whisky wisdom to me. I don't see any peace in here."

"You will after you've had a few of these." He reached for his drink.

"It doesn't give you peace where it really counts," I said as I tapped my heart with two fingers. He knew I was telling the truth, but he wouldn't show it. It would ruin his tough-guy imitation. I took a business card out of my pocket and jotted a note on the back. "Here's where you can find some real peace." I placed it on the table. He ignored me. I pushed away from the table and headed for the exit. I could hardly wait to get outside. My lungs were screaming for fresh air.

Back at the motel I took my second shower of the day. The last thing I wanted was to show up at church smelling like a brewery. I prayed for Jimmy as I shaved in a foggy mirror. "Help him realize there's hope in Jesus."

Only a few folks showed up for church that night: the usual gray-haired men and little old women. I mulled over my sermon for those seasoned saints. That's when the Holy Spirit nudged me.

"You want me to do what?" I argued. "Preach a different sermon?" (Changing sermons at the last minute is like changing horses in midstream.) The Holy Spirit wanted me to preach a full-blown salvation message, which was fine, except those folks had been saved since Noah got off the ark. "Lord, are you sure?" He didn't answer. He didn't have to. "Okay, here we go," I mumbled.

"Stand with me and open your Bible to Matthew 14. I want to preach a sermon tonight on three words Simon Peter prayed when he was on his way down: Lord save me."

At that moment, the door swung open and Jimmy stepped in. He plopped down on the back pew. "Thank you, Holy Spirit. You knew it the whole time."

After the sermon, Jimmy was at the altar on his knees. The pastor was on one side, and I was on the other. The pianist started playing an old church hymn, "I Never Shall Forget the Day."

Late that night I laid in bed and thanked God for orchestrating the whole day. Then the thought occurred to me that God orchestrates every day. So when I woke up the next morning, I expected another nudge . . . from the God who loves people enough to do something about it.

Your ears will hear a word behind you, saying, "This is the way, walk in it, whenever you turn to the right or to the left."
(ISAIAH 30:21 NASB)

TWENTY-SEVEN

The Man Behind the Story

I'm seated at a table interviewing an author. His name is John, the beloved disciple.

"John, may I ask about your book?"

"Yes, please do."

"I think I know the answer, but let me ask, What was your goal while writing your book?"

"That you may believe that Jesus is the Messiah, the Son of God" (John 20:31 NIV).

"And what was your method of persuasion?"

"I intentionally wrote about seven signs that prove Jesus is the Messiah."

"Brilliant. Which signs?"

"Turning water into wine, healing the nobleman's son, healing the invalid at the pool, feeding the five thousand, walking on water, opening the eyes of the blind, and raising Lazarus from death."

"Why did you select those seven signs?"

"I can't take full credit. The Holy Spirit inspired me. These seven signs encompass the scope of mankind's greatest needs."

"What do you mean, exactly?"

"It's all about God's desire to meet the deepest needs in the lives of his people. For example, in Cana, Jesus not only replenished the wine, he restored joy. He restored hope to the nobleman. He restored courage to the invalid. He restored strength to the hungry thousands. He restored Peter's faith. He not only restored the blind man's sight; he restored his vision for the future. And he restored life to Lazarus and gave him a second chance."

"Oh my! I never saw it that way before. So you're saying Jesus has the power to meet every need in the human race."

"Absolutely."

"Would you thank him the next time you see him?"

69

John nods. "He's right here. Thank him yourself." Jesus walks into the room and sits down at the table.

I gulp the air in my throat. "John was just telling me how you restored hope to so many hurting people. You've done the same thing for me. There's no way I can show you how much—"

"Yes, there is."

"There is? How?"

"Share your story."

"My story?"

"Mm-hmm."

"Like the time you forgave all my sins?"

He nodded in agreement.

"I can also tell them about the time when I was so sick, I wondered if I'd make it. But you healed me."

He leaned forward. "Yes. Tell them your story, and if they'll listen long enough, tell them my story too."

"I can tell them about your miraculous birth and your water baptism. And I'll definitely tell them about your death."

He rubbed his left palm with his right thumb. "But make sure they know the reason behind my death. My story has to become their story. They have to know I suffered and died for them, otherwise it's just a narrative. It has to become an experience.

The door opens. You walk in and sit down. Now there are four of us at the table: me, John, you, and Jesus.

John speaks first and tells you his story from two thousand years ago. I speak second and tell you my story over the last fifty years. At last, Jesus speaks. "Come closer," he says.

He gives you a hug. You feel the strength in his arms and the forgiveness in his heart. He whispers your name and says, "I love you."

You break down in tears. "Oh, Jesus. Oh, dear Jesus."

John nods. I wink. Jesus smiles. You got the story. Now it has you too.

These are written that you may believe that
Jesus is the Messiah, the Son of God, and that
by believing you may have life in his name.
(JOHN 20:31 NIV)

TWENTY-EIGHT

Quitter or Winner?

She showed me to the room where I would stay for the week. Then she walked away before I opened the door. Now I know why.

I turned the knob and pushed the door open, but it stopped abruptly. Thump. The room was completely dark, so I reached my hand inside and felt along the wall for a light switch. Flip. Once the light was on, I saw the problem. The door was hitting the side of the bed and couldn't open any farther.

Hmm. The pastor, his wife, and their kids were already in bed. The house was dark and quiet. It was too late to ask for an explanation. Back in those days, I was a slim 130 pounds, so I turned sideways and squeezed between the doorknob and the jam. "Oh, my!" Someone had managed to assemble a full-size bed in a closet. There were no windows, no nightstands, no lamps, no dresser, no mirror; just a bed with a lightbulb hanging overhead.

The headboard stood against one wall, the side of the bed was pushed against the second wall, and the footboard stopped just short of the third wall. That tiny storage space was stacked from floor to ceiling with see-through bins filled with winter clothes, quilts, knitting yarn, and old shoes.

It was late and I was tired. I decided the size of the room wouldn't matter once my eyes were closed, so I pulled back the covers to climb in bed. My heart sank. The bedding had not been changed. Long brown hairs littered the sheets, curled like paisleys in a wild array of patterns. I can deal with a lot of things, but I despise dirty sheets. I didn't cuss, but I thought about spitting in the floor.

I found a handkerchief in my bag and used it like a glove to pick each hair off of the sheets. Then I inverted the pillowcase and dressed for bed, head to toe. The next morning, the four of us sat around the kitchen table for breakfast. A roach fell from the ceiling and landed right in my plate. I swatted it off to one side. They saw it. I saw it. But no one said a word. I ate the rest of my breakfast and prayed for grace.

I laugh about it now, but it wasn't funny back then. Perhaps it was a test to see if I'd quit, throw in the towel, or give up on my calling. That was nearly forty years ago, and I haven't quit yet. Winners never quit and quitters never win.

The challenges I've faced through the years certainly don't compare to the sufferings of the Apostle Paul.

In his letter to the Corinthians he said, "I have . . . been put in prison . . . been whipped . . . faced death again and again . . . was beaten . . . was stoned . . . was shipwrecked . . . faced danger . . . been hungry and thirsty . . . shivered in the cold, without enough clothing to keep me warm" (2 Corinthians 11:23-27 NLT).

But Paul never quit.

Neither did Jesus. He survived the wilderness, resisted temptation, fasted forty days, weathered the storm, bore the brunt of criticism, and suffered cruel beatings at the hands of the Romans. Not only that, he endured the cross with all its humiliation, pain, and torment. Why?

Because he thought we were worth dying for. And that's why we don't quit—because he is worth living for.

I have fought a good fight,
I have finished my course,
I have kept the faith.
(2 TIMOTHY 4:7 KJV)

TWENTY-NINE

Demas the Deserter

The door slammed and woke him up. He rolled left and felt the empty bed. "Roxy, come back." He wrapped a towel around his waist and snatched the door open. "Where are you going?"

She walked fast, wearing his robe and shoes. "Home."

"But you're mine until noon."

"It's past noon," she said without slowing down.

He squinted at the midday sun in disbelief. "You'll be back," he shouted. Neighbors snickered, just like the last time.

He stepped inside and poured a splash of vinegar in a cup of water, squeezed in a handful of grapes, and guzzled it down. His head was splitting. His stomach was churning. Dirty laundry cluttered the floor. Dried puke stank up the joint. He rubbed cold water on his face and looked in the mirror. No wonder she left. His pallid face was a roadmap of wrinkles leading to nowhere. If he could only be the man he used to be.

He found another robe in the top of the closet. When he pulled it down, Paul's letter tumbled out. It had been a long time since he last read it. He sat down on the floor, leaned against the wall, and unrolled the parchment. The ink had faded, but it was still legible. "Dear Demas. Grace and peace in Christ our Lord. I remember your labor of love throughout the churches in Macedonia and your sacrifice for my bonds in Rome. But now I fear for your soul. Your abandonment of me may lead to your abandonment of Christ, for which cause I rest not day or night. . . ." He stopped reading to keep from crying. He pulled the robe over his shoulder, stuffed a silver necklace in his pouch, and headed for the pawn shop.

Thessalonica was all in a stir. Folks in the downtown district were crowding around a street preacher. Catcalls and insults filled the air, but the preacher never flinched. Demas recognized the voice and pushed through the crowd for a better view.

When the sermon ended and the crowd scattered, Demas

approached the preacher. "If I didn't see it with my own eyes, I wouldn't believe it. Markus, the runaway."

"It's been too long, my friend. Did you find what you were looking for in this hellhole?" Mark asked.

Demas shrugged. "I found you."

"But have you found the Lord?"

"Here we are together again after all these years—Markus the runaway and Demas the deserter. What a team." He chuckled to hide his guilt.

"I found my way back. So can you," Mark said.

"It's too late. I'm branded now."

"Branded maybe, but not buried."

"Just say, hypothetically, I wanted back in. What would it take?"

"You know the answer to that. Forsake the world and don't look back. Love God with all your heart."

"It's not as easy as it sounds," Demas said as he hid his money pouch behind his back.

"Easy? Like Christ's crucifixion? Or Paul's imprisonment?"

Demas shrugged and walked away in silence. After the pawn shop, he went straight to Roxy's house.

"Two denarii?" she questioned.

"One for you to come back," Demas said. "And the other, if you bring my clothes with you."

She snatched them out of his hand before he had time to change his mind. "But I'm gone by noon tomorrow."

"Don't remind me."

On their walk back to his house, they heard Markus preaching on a different street corner. Demas skirted around the crowd, but Mark could be heard a block away, "[It's better] to suffer affliction with the people of God, than to enjoy the pleasures of sin for a season" (Hebrews 11:25 KJV).

"Who's that crazy guy?" Roxy said.

Demas stuck his fingers in his ears. "Don't worry about it. Just keep walking."

Do not love the world or the things in the world. If anyone loves the world, the love of the Father is not in him.
(1 John 2:15)

74

THIRTY

My Precious

Two weeks to live. "That's what the doctor said. Fourteen days is hardly enough time to say goodbye to someone you love.

He wanted time to stop, so he took the batteries out of the clock. It didn't stop time, but it did silence the ticking. The constant reminder was more than he could take. Every ticktock was another ratchet to his broken heart.

He sat in a leather chair under a dim light. She lay in a hospice bed at the edge of the shadow. "A hundred seven. A hundred eight." He counted her breaths, wondering which would be her last. Movement under her eyelids indicated a dream, and her inadvertent smile was a sign it was a good dream. Heaven, perhaps? He was reluctant to blink. He might miss something: her last breath, her last word, her last dream, her last anything.

A book lay open in his lap, but he hadn't turned a page in half an hour. It gave him something to look at besides her sunken eyes. She was beautiful even at death's door, perhaps prettier than ever. She was inching closer to heaven; no wonder she looked so peaceful. He wished he felt the same peace.

The pile of tissues on the floor beside his chair was a monument of love. He never seemed to find the right words to tell her how he felt. Poems, cards, flowers, gifts—they all failed. How can anything on earth describe a love that comes from another world? Only tears convey a love unspoken. He pulled another tissue from the box and dried his eyes. The monument grew a little taller and a whole lot sweeter.

A television hung on the wall, but he never touched the remote. Silence was preferred over noise. Besides, no one on the big screen knew how he felt. Comedy was out of place. Commercials were out of touch. News was out of order. Nothing in Hollywood could help him now. Only Jesus understood his broken heart. He picked up his Bible and stacked it on the other book in his lap. The high-lighted verse from yesterday caught his eye again today. "Precious in the sight of the LORD is the death of his saints" (Psalm 116:15 KJV). "Precious?" he whispered. "Lord, help me to see how my wife's death can be precious. If it's precious to you, somehow make it precious to me." He yawned and leaned his head back against the chair. His lips stopped moving, but his prayer continued in his mind. "Lord, make it precious to me."

Soon he was fast asleep and dreamed of a beautiful place: a cloudless sky, a crystal river, a golden city, and the happiest people he'd ever seen. "This must be heaven. But where is Jesus?" An angel, dressed in white, appeared beside him. "Follow me."

The tour was brief but beautiful. He saw stately mansions on top of rolling hills. Children played in meadows of wildflowers. A man and woman laughed together under a trellis of roses. Angels galloped on winged horses through golden fields of grain. Then at last he saw Jesus. He was walking with a woman toward a gazebo surrounded by animals. It looked like something out of a "Snow White" fairytale. Rabbits nibbled grass, squirrels munched acorns, deer flicked their ears, and butterflies danced on daffodils.

As the man drew close, he saw the woman with Jesus was his wife. She was healthy, young, and happy. Their eyes met for the briefest of moments. She raised her right hand, spelled the word *precious* in sign language, and blew him a kiss.

The man woke up from his dream with the morning sun in his face. The long night had ended. He laid his Bible and book on the table beside him and stood up to check on his wife. He knew at first sight. She was already gone. He cupped his hand over his mouth and began to cry. "I never got to tell you goodbye." Then he noticed. Her lips were puckered like she'd just blown a kiss, and her right hand was folded in the sign of an "s"—the last letter of a word.

He spelled out two words with his hands: "My Precious." Then he leaned over and gave her a kiss.

Precious in the sight of the LORD is the death of his saints.
(PSALM 116:15 KJV)

PART TWO

Places to Go

THIRTY-ONE

The Grand Canyon

When the train whistle blew on the Grand Canyon Railway, my wife looked at me with the giddy eyes of a little girl whose dream was about to become true. She leaned toward me and whispered, "Here we go." Even with a (COVID protection) mask on, I could see her smile. Better yet, I could feel it. Her excitement was untethered; her joy, unleashed.

If I've heard her say it once, I've heard her say it a thousand times: "I want to go to the Grand Canyon." The idea popped in her mind when she was seven years old. As a child, she watched the episode of *The Brady Bunch* when they went to the Grand Canyon. The desire to go there got lodged in her mind somewhere between dreams that happen and dreams that don't.

Nearly fifty years later, on a bright morning in the fine month of May, we left every excuse behind at the train depot in Williams, Arizona. As the trained pulled away from the depot, we waved goodbye to total strangers, like we were pioneers headed west on the adventure of a lifetime. (In reality, we were, more than we realized.)

Gift shops and restaurants disappeared behind us as we clipped along down the track between lonely pine trees and lowly juniper bushes. The terrain changed from a small western town to a broad desolate prairie.

Two hours later, we stepped off of the train and onto the brink of one of the seven natural wonders of the world. We crossed the track, climbed a flight of stairs, wound around El Tover Motel, and walked past the Hopi House Gift Shop. And there it was in plain view—a gorge, a ravine, a hole in the ground like we'd never seen before. We edged closer, step by step, to the rim of the Grand Canyon and stood there in total silence.

When I looked at my wife, I saw the kind of tears that puddle in your eyes from staring too long without blinking. A fifty-year dream had come true, and I was the only one there to see it happen. I blurted out, "Is this real?" Then she said what I should've said: "It's so amazing. It looks like a canvas, a painting on a canvas." Then it dawned on me; I know the artist who painted it.

The same God who flung the stars into the night sky, the same God who formed Adam in his hands like a potter molding clay, the same God who unrolled grass like a tarp and tacked it down with daffodils, the same God who spotted the leopard, striped the zebra, and painted the feathers of the peacock is the same God who designed and decorated the rocky wonder in Arizona we call the Grand Canyon.

Scientists tell us the canyon is millions of years old. Time, water, and the process of erosion have formed the canyon into what we see today. Yes, and God, who controls every detail of his creation, supervised the whole thing.

As I stood on the South Rim and watched my wife take in the beauty of God's color-soaked painting, this Scripture unfolded in my mind: "You are worthy, O Lord, to receive glory and honor and power; for You created all things, and by Your will they exist and were created" (Revelation 4:11).

God takes great pleasure in his creation. He's an eternal artist who loves to create beautiful things. He's a designer, a decorator, a builder, an inventor, a composer, and yes—a painter. All of his creations have a certain flare about them. It's his calling card, his fingerprint, his signature. He put red rocks in the Grand Canyon, and he painted aurora in the northern lights. He covered Mount Everest with fresh fallen snow. He splashed Victoria Falls with cascades of wonder, he wrapped colorful coral around the Great Barrier Reef, and he dotted the harbor of Rio de Janeiro with granite mountains that look like giant Hershey's Kisses.

But you don't have to wait fifty years to see one of God's signature masterpieces. You only have to look in the mirror. Look at yourself and be amazed. God formed your nose. He sculpted your ears. Colored your eyes. Fashioned the part in your hair. That's right. The God of wonders saved his best work until last—you!

I am fearfully and wonderfully made.
(Psalm 139:14)

THIRTY-TWO

The Well

Well. That's where Moses sat. That's how Moses felt.

"Moses fled from the face of Pharaoh and dwelt in the land of Midian; and he sat down by a well" (Exodus 2:15).

Midian's well is a lonesome place. It's a single spot in a sea of sand, a place where wanderers sit and wonder what went wrong. It's in the middle of nowhere, but at least it's somewhere to sit when life turns sour. For some, it's a place to remember. For Moses, it was a place to forget.

His best effort at problem-solving had turned into his worst nightmare. So he sat down by the well, depleted and distraught, out of breath and out of luck.

His feet were blistered. His bones were weary. His soul was empty. How did he end up in such a place? He killed one of Pharaoh's foremen and hid his corpse in the sand, hoping no one would find out. Someone did. They always do.

His trek through the wilderness was his attempt to "get out of Dodge" before getting caught. He escaped from Pharaoh, but he couldn't escape from himself. Guilt dogged every step. Condemnation hounded every thought. After he crawled through a desert of blame, he collapsed at the well of shame. His paper-thin shoes clung to his swollen feet, and his threadbare cloak hid his face from the wrath of the sun.

You've been to the well, haven't you? The deep place in the ground that represents a deep place in your life. The place where you sit down because you've given up.

Moses sat by his well. We plop beside ours. When's the last time you said, "Oh well"?

"Oh well, I failed the entrance exam." Plop.

"Oh well, I lost my job again." Plop.

"Oh well, the x-ray shows cancer." Plop.

"Oh well, the husband wants a divorce." Plop.

Wells and plops are desert companions. Where you find one, you find the other.

Moses thought the well was his finish line; instead, it was his start line. Life wasn't over for him. It was time for a new beginning. At the well, Moses rescued Jethro's daughter from some rogue shepherds. That rescue led to an invitation to dinner. The meal led to a marriage. The marriage led to family. The family led to a future.

Eventually, God sent Moses back to Egypt with an assignment—rescue the others. This time Moses did it God's way, in God's time, with God's approval, and for God's glory. And it worked. Ten plagues later, God's people crossed the Red Sea and headed for the Promised Land.

We'd all like to bury our mistakes in the sand, like Moses, but there's not enough sand in Sinai. Thankfully, there's enough grace at Calvary. That's the place where "Oh well" turns into "Oh my."

I focus on this one thing: forgetting the past
and looking forward to what lies ahead.
(PHILIPPIANS 3:13 NLT)

THIRTY-THREE

Main Street, U.S.A.

Ever since I was a kid, I believed the happiest place on earth was the Magic Kingdom. It's the only place I know of where you can tiptoe through a haunted mansion, cruise through an alligator infested jungle, and soar through a mountain of space all in the same day; and that doesn't include photo ops with Mickey Mouse, getting lost on Tom Sawyer's Island, or watching fireworks over Cinderella's Castle. It'll take your breath away.

I've been to Disney World many times. It's my family's go-to destination for vacation. Yet, in the place where magic happens every day and dreams are sprinkled with pixie dust, there was one wish left unfulfilled. My wife and I wanted to experience that euphoric moment known as *rope drop.*

What is rope drop? It's a once-in-a-lifetime thrill for hard-core fans who are willing to do whatever it takes to stand on Main Street U.S.A. when the park opens. You have to get up before the crack of dawn if you want to see it. Skip breakfast. Drive like a maniac. Run through the ticket station. Jump on the monorail. Sprint down the exit ramp. Dart under the train depot. Then shimmy as close as you can to the Emporium. Don't be surprised if hundreds of other fans have already beat you to it.

Years ago, my wife and I decided to make it happen. Let me describe it to you. Cinderella's Castle stood in front of us, adorned in all her glory. Magical spires reached to the heavens, brooding over a clean swept, freshly painted, completely empty park—waiting for the first laughs of the day. We stood behind the rope, corralled like wild stallions, with hundreds of other Disney-crazed fans. Half-sleepy tots wore Cinderella dresses and Mickey Mouse ears. Dads carried backpacks, diaper bags, and video equipment. Moms slathered suntan lotion on their children from head to toe.

Festivals of balloons waved in the Florida breeze, and the smell of chocolate fudge oozed out of the confectionary. Just beyond the castle, a world of make-believe friends waited to welcome us: Peter Pan in Neverland, one-eyed pirates in the Caribbean, and seven little dwarfs in a diamond mine. We bounced on our toes with excitement.

Then it happened like a New Year's countdown: three, two, one. Zip-a-dee-doo-dah filled the air and the rope dropped to the pavement. We were off to the races. Vacationers scattered in every direction, sprinting toward their favorite rides.

We left every care behind. No more office work, homework, or housework. No more yard work. Don't even say the word *work*. For five days the only thing that mattered was fun, fun, and more fun.

After dancing with Sebastian at the bottom of the sea and hiding in a briar patch with Br'er Rabbit, we stormed the barn with Goofy and hid from the Mad Hatter in spinning cups and saucers.

But as you know, all vacations come to an end.

"O, bother," says Winnie-the-Pooh.

"It's back to work again," says Eeyore.

When I got home, it dawned on me—I'm way up here in Virginia and the Magic Kingdom is way down there in Florida, but that doesn't mean I can't enjoy my day.

"Trust me," says Aladdin.

"There's a whole new world to explore," says Ariel.

Since this is the day the Lord has made, I'm going to rejoice and be glad in it (Psalm 118:24), even on a workday.

Besides, the Magic Kingdom has rope drop every day of the year. Why can't I have my own rope drop? I can and I will.

Now every morning when I pull the cover off to one side and place my feet on the floor, I determine my day starts with rope drop. It's my own personal adventure. The Lord is with me. Angels are around me. The day is before me. This can be my "Zip-a-Dee-Doo-Dah" day if I choose for it to be. And so it is.

My friend, don your faith glasses. Slather on the peace of God. Breathe in the joy of the Lord. Sing your song. Dance your dance. Your morning just started. The rope dropped.

This is the day the LORD has made;
We will rejoice and be glad in it.
(PSALM 118:24)

THIRTY-FOUR

The Burning Bush

The cool night gave way to the morning sun as the slumbering flock awoke to their master's call. His plan for the day was a distant trek to look for greener pastures. With an early start, he'd reach his destination by afternoon. The search for new territory was more about the shepherd than the sheep. They were content. He was the one empty on the inside.

Moses trudged along, a step at a time, pretending to enjoy his work. In reality, his life was as stale and crusty as the bread in his pocket. Nothing excited him anymore. His day consisted of hooves and horns, lambs and rams. Moses spat on the ground and sighed, wondering if God even knew where he was. He had no idea how soon his lonely heart would be warmed by God's holy presence.

"What? The bush burns with fire but is not consumed. How can that be?" Moses thought.

Curiosity drew the part-time shepherd off his predictable path. He inched closer for a better look, not knowing the shrub was looking back at him. A face in the fire?

The flame broke the silence and called his name. "Moses, Moses!" (Exodus 3:4). "Take your shoes off. This is holy ground."

He backed out of his shoes and stood barefooted on the cold ground. Had he trespassed on some ancient burial ground? No. The mysterious Voice offered an invitation, not an eviction. And nothing would buffer the hallowed moment—not even shoe leather.

"I've heard the cry of my people in Egypt. I'm sending you to deliver them from bondage."

"But who am I that I should go? . . . But I don't know your name . . . But they won't listen to me . . . But I don't know what to say . . . But I'm not good with words . . . But I'm not cut out for this . . . But you should send someone else . . . But . . . But . . . But . . ."

"Shh!" The fire crackled. "I know who you are. It's time you know who I am. Let me introduce myself, so in turn, you can introduce me to my people in Egypt. They have forgotten the God of their fathers. I Am—that's who I am. I am the fire that goes before you. I am the wind that blows behind you. I am the rock that stands beneath you. I am the God who reigns above you. I am the truth who speaks within you.

"Today you set out to discover a new place. Instead, you discovered a new you. And more than that, you have discovered me. I will use you to humble Pharaoh and the gods of Egypt.

"Don't question whether or not I can use you. I used this scraggly thornbush, didn't I, with all its prickly points and flimsy branches? I will use you too, in spite of all your pointed objections and flimsy excuses.

"Now, pick up your staff, put on your shoes, and set out for Egypt. Your destiny awaits. And when the enemy stands before you, and you wonder who's in your corner, just remember, I Am."

This is what you shall say to the sons of Israel:
I AM has sent me to you.
(Exodus 3:14 NASB)

THIRTY-FIVE

Eighteen Miles Away

Eighteen miles is not too far if it's the last leg of a long journey. Right? What's eighteen miles if you're driving to a pebbled beach in the sun with your lounge chair in tow and a lemonade in hand? What's eighteen miles to a log cabin in the woods with a fire on the hearth and snow on the ground? Better yet, what's eighteen miles to a tropical island with a private cabana and a hammock swaying between palm trees.

On the flip side, eighteen miles to a gas station when you're running on fumes is a long stretch. Agree? What about eighteen miles to the rest room when you need to . . . (cough, cough)? Say no more, but eighteen miles is too far.

What if I told you that you were only eighteen miles from your next miracle? How would you feel? Pretty good? And so it was for the nation of Israel in the days of Joshua. They were eighteen miles from a miracle of national proportions and didn't know it.

Here's what happened. "It was the harvest season, and the Jordan was overflowing its banks. But as soon as the feet of the priests who were carrying the Ark touched the water at the river's edge, the water above that point began backing up a great distance away at a town called Adam, which is near Zarethan. And the water below that point flowed on to the Dead Sea until the riverbed was dry. Then all the people crossed over near the town of Jericho" (Joshua 3:15-16 NLT).

Crossing the Jordan River was a miracle indeed, yet it was so different from the miracles they had seen in the past, which tells me that God is not locked into doing new things in old ways. He has a big imagination, and I think he takes great pleasure in surprising his children. "It is God's privilege to conceal things" (Proverbs 25:2 NLT).

Forty years earlier, when the nation of Israel crossed the Red Sea, Moses held up his rod and God held up his end of the bargain.

Before you had time to say, "Give me my camera; I want a picture of this," a dry path sliced through the middle of the sea with walls of water piled up on both sides. The red light turned green and God's people put the pedal to the metal—no waiting required.

But forty years later, under Joshua, it was a miracle of a different sort. There was no rod of Moses this time. Instead, God ordered the priests to carry the sacred chest between them and walk into the edge of the Jordan River. No wind blew. No path appeared. Nothing happened. "Okay God, we obeyed you. Where's our miracle?"

You've been there, right? You prayed, you trusted, you believed, but nothing happened.

Wrong. Something did happen, eighteen miles away.

While the priests stood knee-deep in the water and the people stood impatiently on the shore, God worked on their behalf eighteen miles to the north. An avalanche of sorts dammed up the riverbed near the city of Adam, causing water to back up from that point northward. The waters south of the dam, from Adam to Jericho, receded like water draining out of a bathtub. How long did it take for the riverbed to drain dry? Perhaps all day.

Now we see what happened. Their initial step of faith did result in a miracle, but it was out of sight, eighteen miles to the north. They had to stand in faith for hours until knee-deep water became ankle-deep, and ankle-deep water became dry land.

Just like me, you've taken steps of faith and wondered why nothing happened. The pain didn't subside. The cancer didn't vanish. The money didn't appear. You thought nothing happened, because you didn't see the result right away. But something did happen, my friend. Heaven heard, God moved, and angels were sent on assignment. The answer is on the way, but you can't see it.

So now is the time to stand still, to wait, and to trust. Don't back up. Don't blame God. Don't throw a hissy fit. The God of surprises has something up his sleeve. And remember, he has big sleeves.

Although today you stand knee-deep in problems, tomorrow you'll stand in the Promised Land. It's only eighteen miles away.

For we walk by faith, not by sight.
(2 Corinthians 5:7)

THIRTY-SIX

The Gorge

We had a secret hideout when I was growing up. It was several blocks away from home, behind an old store. Our hideout was a deep ravine surrounded by a thicket of trees. I still remember my first visit.

The ravine was a circular gorge, unnatural and unearthly. We kids thought it was evidence of alien life forms. It looked like a meteor crashed there, or better yet, a Martian spaceship landed and left a footprint.

A menacing tree stood on the rim of the ravine and fanned out over the depression like strategic camouflage. One sturdy limb stretched across the expanse and supported a tug rope that dangled to the floor of the gorge. A large knot hung at the end of the rope, tempting any kid brave enough to ride across the abyss.

"You gonna ride it?" he asked.

"Who, me? No way!"

"You're a scaredy-cat."

"No I'm not."

"Yes you are."

"I'll ride it, if you ride it."

"Let's ride it together, at the same time."

"Are you sure it'll hold both of us?"

We skidded down the slope and walked out to the dangling knot.

I looked up at the top of the rope and saw a big knot. "Who climbed out there and tied it?"

"I dunno, but he must of been crazy," my friend said.

"And you're crazy if you think I'm gonna ride on it; it might break."

"Oh, come on. Help me pull it to the top."

We each held the rope and climbed on all fours up the wall of the ravine. I thought it was a death trap and that I'd never see the light of another day. Once we made it to the top of the ridge, we decided to sit spider-legged on the knot with the smallest kid on top. That was me.

He took two steps and leaped off the ledge. I screamed my guts out and held on for dear life. We swooped down the gorge with the speed of a pterodactyl diving for its prey. Skimming near the ground, the rope continued upwards to the other side. It dawned on me that this death-defying feat wasn't over yet. Several more times our momentum carried us up the sides of the gorge and plunged us into the depths of the ravine.

Tears streaked down the sides of my face as I squealed, "Jesus. Help me, Jesus." Nothing brings on desperate prayer like the thought of meeting your Maker.

Years later, I revisited that old hideout and was shocked at the sight. What I thought was a deep gorge, as a child, wasn't deep at all. The tree was medium sized, the limb was nothing spectacular, and the rope and the knot looked meek and mild. I shook my head in disbelief, "What was I afraid of? It doesn't look so dangerous after all."

Now I realize it's all a matter of perspective. Big challenges for kids aren't big challenges for adults. Your greatest troubles of bygone years are small potatoes to you today. And the daunting challenges you face right now will look like child's play after a while. It's all about perspective. And from God's "eye in the sky," every problem is a small problem.

What lesson did I learn from the gorge? One of these days you'll look back on life and tell someone else, "It wasn't so bad after all."

Be strong and do not give up.
(2 Chronicles 15:7 NIV)

THIRTY-SEVEN

Green Pastures

Strap on your boots. Tie them nice and tight. Spray on bug repellent. Grab a bottle of water. Now follow me. We're going on a hike. A hike to where? The Valley of the Shadow of Death. This is your last chance to turn back. Are you in or out?

Good, you're in. Let's get moving. The dawn is just breaking. This is the same trek shepherds have walked for thousands of years, including David the psalmist. It'll be hot and humid later today, so enjoy the morning temperature while you can. Dry rocks crackle beneath our feet as we descend the southwestern slope of Bethlehem heading for the outskirts of Gedor.

For the next two hours, all you hear is the crunch of footsteps along the Judean hills, the solitary cry of a blackbird, and the labored breathing of someone slightly out of shape. Knees ache. Shoulders slump. Sweat drips.

"Can we take a break?" you say.

"Sure, but not right here. There's a better place up ahead."

The mountains surrounding us are sun-blistered and burnt brown from centuries of harsh, arid weather. The path beneath our feet is a drab, dull gray. Dust stirs with every step. But as we near the valley floor, we see a sight for sore eyes—a patch of something green.

This is the place I told you about. It looks like an oasis in the desert. I sit on the ground and lean against a big rock. You lie flat on your back and let out a sigh of relief. You're tempted to do "snow angels" in the lush grass.

"Wow, I love this place," you say. "What's it called so I can remember it later?"

I unroll an ancient scroll containing the hymns of David and find the 23rd. "The Lord is my shepherd, I lack nothing. He makes me lie down in green pastures" (Psalm 23:1-2 NIV).

"Ahh, so this is Green Pastures? I never knew it was a real place."

91

"I don't know it's proper name, but I call it the resting place."

"Well, whatever it's called, it arrived just in time. Honestly, I've had about all I can take for one day. I don't think I could've gone any farther."

We open our leather satchels and enjoy a midmorning snack. The cheese is from Jerusalem, the grapes are from Jericho, and the pomegranate juice was squeezed fresh this morning by yours truly.

A lazy cloud floats overhead and provides needed relief from the sun. The temperature drops several degrees, and a whispery breeze dries the sweat on the back of your neck. This is a good time to shake the sand out of your boots and put lotion on your feet.

"I love this place too," I say. "It's a parable of life. The Lord knows we need times of rest, moments of reprieve, and a place to catch our breath. When we need it the most, he leads us to green pastures, especially when the road has been rough and rocky. It's a mini-vacation, a brain massage."

Green pastures come in many forms: an unexpected day off of work, a leisure walk in the park, a quiet nap at the rest stop, or a date night as grandparents watch the kids.

You rub your hand along the top of the grass and wiggle your toes in the carpet of green. A tear of appreciation wells up in your eye. "I love this place; it reminds me how much the Good Shepherd loves me. The shade, the breeze, the grass—they are all tokens of his love. I never realized it until now. He has proven his love for me in so many ways. How can I ever thank him enough?"

We have a few more minutes to rest before we head north, so I decide to play a song from my iTunes list. We close our eyes and listen.

> *Peace, peace, wonderful peace,*
> *Coming down from the Father above!*
> *Sweep over my spirit forever, I pray*
> *In fathomless billows of love!*
> (WARREN D. CORNELL AND OLIVER W. COOPER)[1]

> *My people will dwell in a peaceful habitation,*
> *In secure dwellings, and in quiet resting places.*
> (ISAIAH 32:18)

THIRTY-EIGHT

Still Waters

Okay, I'm ready to continue our hike."

"Let's go," you say as you hoist your backpack over one shoulder.

I smile and nod, wondering if you're really ready for the next leg of our journey. I'm impressed by your enthusiasm, but I also know it will be tougher than yesterday.

We turn north and follow the path of the dry valley floor. Within a few minutes the green pastures behind us are out of sight and so are the clouds. The snake-like path wanders before us, left and right, but the scenery never changes—barren nothingness.

The sun approaches high noon and beams down directly into the rocky basin. Infernal heat reflects off of the canyon walls and slow-cooks us in a Judean cauldron. We're stuck in a microwave and have sweated until we can't sweat anymore. You hold your canteen upside down and show me it's completely empty, not a drop left.

"No worries," I say.

"No worries?" You halfway chuckle. "I don't see a 7-Eleven or a Starbucks close by. Can you get water from these rocks like Moses?"

"You'll have more water than you can handle in about ten minutes."

"I gotta see this magic trick."

"It's not magic."

We traipse along one step at a time. I notice you keep looking at the mountain ridge on both sides. It resembles the spine of a stegosaurus.

"I'm going to faint if we don't get some water soon," you remind me.

I hold back my grin as we round the bend to the left, waiting for your reaction.

"Oh my heavens!" You throw both hands in the air. "It's Christmas morning."

"Yep, I've been here before."

Growing out of sheer rock is the prettiest little broom bush you've ever seen. From under its roots flow a steady stream of water that trickles down the rock and pools in a shallow place.

"Is it safe to drink?"

"You betcha."

Your backpack slides off your shoulder and hits the dirt behind your feet. You're on your knees in two seconds flat with cool water in both hands.

"It's happy hour."

My suppressed giggle sneaks out in spurts of joy. Water pours off your chin, trails down your arms, and drips off your elbows. You let out a belch, and we both laugh out loud.

"Here. Fill 'em up." I toss you our canteens.

The gurgling noise sounds like music to our ears. For a few moments we forget we're sitting in the middle of a desolate wilderness. We cross our legs and chat like we're vacationing on a Caribbean beach.

"It's time for our lesson of the day," I say.

I unroll David's twenty-third Psalm and read the next line.

"He leads me beside the still waters" (Psalm 23:2).

Isn't it comforting to realize our Shepherd knows the terrain before us? When we're bone dry and can't see hope on the horizon, he never worries, because he knows what's up ahead.

He knows the doctor's report before we do. He knows how the interview will go. He knows the weight on our shoulders, the emptiness in our soul, and the worried look in our eyes. He also knows where the water hole is, and that's where he's leading us. Don't doubt him. He's been this way before.

But He knows the way that I take.
(JOB 23:10)

THIRTY-NINE

The Valley of the Shadow

On the third morning of our hike, we wake up to the noise of travelers headed in the opposite direction. They stop just long enough to offer some advice.

"Take this rod and staff with you. If you plan to cross the valley today, you'll need them. Believe me."

I nod, knowing he's telling the truth. I've walked that way before.

You finish your morning coffee without saying a word. It's your first trek through the gorge. You've heard harrowing stories about the place—Death Valley. Soon our friends bid us adieu and continue on their way.

"Douse the fire," I say. "Time is wasting, and we've got a long way to go before the sun sets."

Walking is easier today than the last two days. It's all downhill. You follow me from two strides back. Your quiet demeanor tells me you've got something on your mind. A lizard darts across our path, and you take it as an opportunity to open up. "How can anything survive out here in the middle of nowhere?"

"You'd be surprised how many animals live in this barren place."

"I haven't seen anything except a few vultures and one lizard."

"Oh, there are plenty of animals out here. They're hard to spot. They blend in with the terrain."

"What kind of animals?"

I'm reluctant to tell you. "Wolves, coyotes, jackals, and snakes."

Your eyebrows peak and you start looking high and low.

"Don't worry. They mostly prowl at night. It's daylight now."

Within a few hours we arrive at the valley floor. It's nothing like the wide, plush valleys you're accustomed to back home. This is a V-shaped gorge with a narrow path, surrounded by impassable mountains on both sides. We have to look straight up to see the sky.

I point out some well-hidden caves and camouflaged dens. "In olden times, thugs and thieves would hide in these holes and wait for unsuspecting travelers."

We stop long enough to read the story of the Good Samaritan. "A certain *man* went down from Jerusalem to Jericho, and fell among thieves, who stripped him of his clothing, wounded *him*, and departed, leaving *him* half dead" (Luke 10:30).

"Ah, it makes sense now," you say. "When we're in the valley, we are vulnerable to the enemy's attack. If you faint here, you're as good as dead."

I hand you the shepherd's staff, and then I lay down on my back in the dirt.

"What are you doing?"

"Pretend I'm injured, bleeding, and half dead. Now help me up."

You reach down with your hand.

"No. Use the staff."

You extend it toward me, and I wrap the crook around my shoulder. "Ok, give it a try. Pull." Within moments, I'm back on my feet again. "See. That wasn't so hard."

You grin. "Psalm 23, right? 'Your rod and Your staff, they comfort me.'"

"Yep. That's how David restored his sheep. Have you ever needed God to restore you, to help you get back on your feet?"

"Oh yeah, plenty of times."

"Me too."

"Hey, do you mind if I hold on to this staff a little longer? You never know, I might need it again."

"Sure, but if we don't hurry along, we'll have to spend the night in this place, and believe me, neither one of us want to do that."

It's only midafternoon, but the sun sets fast when you're in a valley. We pick up the pace as I hum an old tune.

I am determined to hold out to the end,
Jesus is with me, on Him I can depend.
(C. S. HAMILTON AND T. P. HAMILTON)[1]

Your rod and Your staff, they comfort me.
(PSALM 23:4)

FORTY

Almost Home

On the last night of our hike, we sit around the campfire and eat cooked meat on metal skewers. The moonlight is dim. The shadows are dark. The valley floor is cold.

"I'm proud of you. Thanks for coming on this wilderness trek with me. I hope you don't regret it."

"No, not at all," you say. "As a matter of fact, I've learned a lot of lessons I'll never forget."

Your hair is pressed flat to your head from the hat you wore all day, and your eyes glint in the light of the fire. "Would you do it again?"

"Well, yeah. But not next week. I need an air-conditioner, a fresh shower, and a Serta mattress."

I giggle. "Ain't that the truth?"

"What was that?" you ask as your head snaps to the left.

I grab a stick from the fire and stand up. "I'm not sure, but it didn't sound good." We peer into the shadows looking for whatever just growled. "Give me the rod."

"The what?"

"The rod. The shepherd's rod," I say without taking my eyes off of that thing staring at me in the dark.

You scrounge around in your backpack but can't find it.

"Hurry. I think it's a mountain lion or a cougar." Its eyes glow a reflective green. Its growl is intense. It could pounce at any moment.

"It's not here. I can't find it."

"No. The other bag." I turn my head and point.

"Screeeech!" The big cat leaps out of the shadows and knocks me to the ground. I drop my torch and roll to one side.

"Help! Get this thing off of me." It's claws rip through my jacket. Hot blood runs down my back.

You hurl the rod at close range—THWACK—and hit it right on the head. It yelps and scurries back into the shadows.

"You're bleeding. Don't move."

I'm face down in the dirt, grimacing in pain. You find the first aid kit and clean the wound. After applying ointment and salve, you bandage me up and help me get in our tent.

"You saved my life."

"I almost cost you your life. I couldn't find that rod."

"But you did find it, just in time, and used it like a pro. That was courageous of you."

"God had to help me. I didn't know what to do."

I squeeze out a giggle.

"What's funny?"

"I almost died in the Valley of Death."

You shake your head in disbelief. "Wow, this is crazy."

The next morning, you help me to my feet. "Let's get out of here," I say. "We're almost home. It's only a half-day's walk."

The Judean hills are peaceful in the morning light. Puffy clouds dot the skies, and a flock of birds soar in the wind.

"I thought of another lesson we learned last night."

"Let me guess: Bring a shotgun next time."

I snicker. "Don't make me laugh. It hurts. No, a lesson about the ointment and salve you put on my back."

"What about it?"

"Psalm 23:5 says, 'You anoint my head with oil.' It wasn't my head you anointed, but still, we learned the value of healing oil. I could've gotten an infection without it, or worse."

"No wonder Jesus is called the Good Shepherd. His word repels the enemy, like the rod. His Spirit heals our wounds, like the oil."

"Look." I point up the dusty road. "A sight for sore eyes, and a sore back."

"Home, sweet home."

I will dwell in the house of the LORD forever.
(PSALM 23:6)

FORTY-ONE

Standing in the Dark

Son, today you're going to learn not to be afraid of the dark."

I had the same fear when I was his age, and I wanted him to overcome it early on so it wouldn't plague him all his life.

The two of us went into the darkest room in the house. It was a small bathroom with no windows.

"Here's what we are going to do. I'm going to shut the door and turn off the light. The two of us are going to stand here in the dark together until you realize there's nothing to be afraid of. Don't worry, I'll hold your hand the whole time, and whenever you want, I'll turn the light on. Okay?"

"Okay."

I flipped the switch, and before it got dark, he said, "Turn the light on."

I turned it on. "Son, that's not the plan. We have to stand in the dark for a while until you are no longer afraid. Okay?"

"Okay."

I turned the light off again. He pressed his little body right up against me.

"Daddy, there's a black cat." (We didn't own a cat.)

I turned the light on. "That's not a cat. That's a flower pot your mother brought in here for decoration."

I turned the light off. "There are two eyeballs looking at me."

I turned the light on. "They're not eyeballs. They're doorknobs on the cabinet door."

I turned the light off. "Dad, there's a monster in the corner."

I flipped the light on again. "That's not a monster. That's the shower curtain. You're not afraid of a shower curtain, are you?"

At last, with the light off, he giggled in the dark. "I'm not afraid of that. It's just the trash can."

I turned the light on, and sure enough, he was pointing to the trash can. "I'm proud of you, son. You did it."

As we grow older, it's not the monster in the corner we're afraid of. It's the doctor's report, the economic indicators, and the talk of pandemic viruses that makes our skin crawl.

Fear is an enemy we have to overcome these days. Every news channel, every CDC report, and every forecaster has us biting our fingernails. People's nerves are shot. Anxiety disorder and panic attacks have become the norm in America.

But I have great news. 2 Timothy 1:7 says, "God has not given us a spirit of fear, but of power and of love and of a sound mind."

Here's a case in point. With the lights off, Elisha's servant saw the Syrian army had them surrounded. Fear gripped his heart. Anxiety controlled his mind. "This is hopeless, my master! What are we to do?" (2 Kings 6:15 NASB).

Elisha wasn't afraid, because he knew God was in control. He prayed for his servant. "'Lord, please, open his eyes so that he may see.' And the Lord opened the servant's eyes, and he saw; and behold, the mountain was full of horses and chariots of fire all around" (2 Kings 6:17 NASB).

When the light came on, Elisha's servant saw what he couldn't see in the dark: an army of angels had them surrounded and there was no need to fear.

Most of our life is spent in the dark: dark valleys, dark shadows, dark times, dark clouds, and dark nights. But God's light shines brightest in dark places.

"The light shines in the darkness, and the darkness can never extinguish it" (John 1:5 NLT).

My son learned not to be afraid of the dark for two good reasons. First, his father never let go of his hand. Second, his father was in control of the light switch.

As children of the Most High God, we no longer panic in the dark; instead, we keep our hand in his hand and giggle until the light comes on.

Therefore we will not fear, though the earth give way and
the mountains fall into the heart of the sea.
(PSALM 46:2 NIV)

FORTY-TWO

Ezel Rock

Long before road signs were posted on poles to give direction, a rock formation stood in the open field near Jerusalem. The locals called it Ezel. Perhaps I could call it Farewell Rock. I have no idea what it looked like, but I like to think it was easy to identify.

"Go to the rock and turn left."

"Which rock?"

"Don't worry. You can't miss it."

David sat down and waited at Ezel Rock, wondering which way his life would turn. Would he turn toward Jerusalem and live in the court, or would he head for the hills and live in the caves? Only time would tell and, of course, a secret sign from his best friend, Jonathan.

"The day after tomorrow, toward evening, go to the place where you hid when this trouble began, and wait by the stone Ezel" (1 Samuel 20:19 NIV).

You've sat in the shadows of Ezel, haven't you? Like David, you've wondered about your future. "Is it benign?" "Will I lose my job?" "Can I afford to retire?" Ezel is where you pace the floor. It's where minutes creep and worries collect. It's where black hairs turn gray and gray hairs turn loose. Ezel is the birthplace of sweaty palms and sleepless nights.

David hid at Ezel and waited . . . and wondered . . . and worried. Then he spotted Jonathan in the distance. They had arranged a secret sign in case murderous King Saul tagged along with evil intent. Jonathan pretended to practice archery. He flexed the bow and let the arrow fly.

"Go get it," Jonathan said to the lad. He watched the little boy scamper through the grass, arms flailing and legs kicking. Grasshoppers jumped, butterflies danced, and the grass swayed in the wake of the chase. In Jonathan's mind, all he could see was David running away, never to return.

"I found it," the boy said, holding it high over his head like a trophy.

Jonathan reached for another arrow. The quiver in his hand echoed the quiver in his voice. "Get ready. Here comes the next one." It was the moment of truth. A shallow shot signals David to come to Jerusalem. A long shot signals David to run for the hills. His fingers trembled. His soul shuttered. He notched the arrow on the string and fought back the tears. He aimed higher and farther than before. The flight of this arrow meant farewell to his friend. David would no longer dine in the halls of the palace. He would live his days like a rogue on the run, hiding in caves, scrounging for sustenance.

Jonathan groaned as the arrow sailed over the boy's head. Cupping his hands, he shouted a masked message to David, "It's beyond you. Run. Run. Don't look back." The lad thought Jonathan spoke to him. David knew better. In the shadow of Ezel Rock, he dropped his head. He heard the message. He knew the meaning. It was time to skedaddle. It wasn't the news David wanted to hear, but life is like that sometimes.

Perhaps the news you heard was not the news you wanted to hear. "Sorry, ma'am, but we can't find a heartbeat. Your baby died." "Sorry, sir, but the layoff is mandatory. Don't come to work on Monday." "Sorry, but your application was not accepted at this time." Ezel is a hard place, hard as a rock.

For what it's worth, Ezel wasn't David's destiny. It was only a temporary detour. In a matter of time, Saul died on Gilboa and David reigned in Jerusalem.

Bad news today doesn't stop good news tomorrow. So when things take a turn for the worse, just remember, detours don't define your life, destiny does.

He makes everything work out according to his plan.
(EPHESIANS 1:11 NLT)

FORTY-THREE

Lonely Street

This is the story of a lonely man who lives on Lonely Street. Tall buildings line both sides of the narrow strip he calls home. Nightfall covers the place like a thick tarp. His backyard is cloaked under dark shadows. His front yard consists of murky rain puddles. One streetlight flickers, barely, like his hope: on again, off again. The sidewalk is worn to a nub, just enough to stump his toe. Cracks on the asphalt lead to the gutter. His only companions are a black cat and a sewer rat.

Cold brick walls hide the coldhearted people who live in the apartments. Their doors are bolted, windows closed, and curtains drawn. They'd rather not look at the horrid place he calls home. No one knows he's there. Even if they did, they wouldn't care. Lonely Street is where he lives, but it can hardly be called living. It's something less than that. He's breathing, but not really living.

A directional sign stands on a rusty pole a block away. The faded letters tell a lie. It says, "One Way." But he's traveled it both ways, up and down, and it's lonely on both ends. If he screams, no one answers. If he yells, it won't matter. He tried. It didn't work. His tears go unseen. His pain goes unnoticed.

The rain puddle is his reflection pool. He closes his eyes and pretends to be in a better place: a Japanese garden with spotted koi fish, a lush forest with hidden waterfalls, or a crowded beach with happy people. When he opens his eyes, he sees the same old pothole full of dirty water, too dirty to see his reflection, and that's probably a good thing. No one else sees him. Why should he see himself?

Two blocks down, on the left, there's a ladder. It's bolted to the building. It's a fire escape. There are thirteen steps that lead to a scaffold. He climbed to the top and knocked on the steel door. No one answered, so he climbed down. The sign said it was an escape route, but he realized there's no escape from Lonely Street.

There's a metal grate in the middle of the road. Steam rises up on cold nights. It stinks, but it's warm. He lays sticks on the grate and closes his eyes, pretending it's a campfire. He says it smells like roasted marshmallows if you wait long enough or hotdogs if you dream big. When his imagination runs out, he's still hungry and still sitting over a sewer exhaust.

He has a choice of a hundred beds, but they're all the same, hard as concrete. There are fifty square pads on this sidewalk, and fifty more on that sidewalk. He's tried them all and prefers none. The best place to sleep is the trash bin. Trash is softer than concrete, and the side walls block the wind. He says it's like a motel in there. Well, it's not a nice motel. There's no room service, but if you scrounge around, you might find a snack.

Tomorrow is his favorite day. It's the day the red door opens. There's an old cross that hangs over their door. Once a week he goes inside and takes a shower and eats a hot meal. But the best part of tomorrow are the hugs from the people who let him inside. Those hugs remind him that there are a few people in the world who still care—the people who live beneath the old rugged cross.

For I was hungry and you gave me something to eat, I was thirsty and you gave me something to drink, I was a stranger and you invited me in.
(MATTHEW 25:35 NIV)

FORTY-FOUR

Mount Carmel

*W*hile trudging up the mountain pass, he stopped long enough to lean against a pine tree and shake dirt out of his sandals. The pebbles on the path weren't his biggest problem; it was the voices in his head that slowed him down. Doubtful thoughts ricocheted back and forth in his mind like a pinball machine.

Stubborn sunrays pierced through the tangled branches above him and reminded him that no rain was in the forecast. The dry ground beneath his feet cracked open, waiting for a single drop of water. It hadn't rained in a long time, a very long time.

He sighed, put his sandals back on, and plodded up the mountain toward the lookout. His walking stick steadied his steps, but his mind stumbled over the question, "How many more times do I have to do this?"

He'd always been a faithful servant of Elijah: running errands, cooking meals, building fires, and fetching supplies. And he did so without complaint. But this request was more than redundant. It was ridiculous. Six times Elijah had sent him to look for rain clouds. Six times the servant climbed to the top of the mountain. Six times the report came back—no rain (1 Kings 18:43).

He broke into the clearing on the top of Mount Carmel and looked in every direction. To the northeast the valley stretched fourteen miles to the foothills. The lengthy drought had turned the lush valley of Jezreel into a wasteland. He scanned the skies to the south where coastal cities baked like fish over hot coals. Caught between the blazing sun and the balmy beach, they sweltered in a sauna of high heat and dry winds. He placed his hand on his brow and looked due west across the Mediterranean Sea. A few ships on the horizon morphed into a blur as the heat of the sun sucked the life from the salty waters.

He dropped his head in disbelief. "Not again." Disappointment is a hard pill to swallow, especially with no hope to wash it down. He could hardly fathom telling Elijah for the seventh time that there was no rain in the forecast. He placed his hand at his brow and scanned the skies a second time. He saw a little something. He rubbed his eyes and looked again, just to be sure.

"Hmm. I think it's a cloud. If it is, it's an interesting one. It's shaped like a man's hand. Should I even mention it to Elijah? It's so small, so insignificant."

The trip down the path was a little easier, with a bit of good news to share. But he was reluctant to tell Elijah what he'd seen.

"Umm. I think I saw something, but I'm not quite sure."

"Spit it out. What was it?"

"Out in the distance, a strange little cloud, kind of shaped like a man's hand" (1 Kings 18:44, author's paraphrase).

"Whoop! Glory! That's all I needed to hear. We better get off this mountain. Here comes a gully washer."

"Wait, Elijah. Don't get so excited. It was just a small cloud. I'm not even sure it's headed this way."

"The devil is a lie. That's my cloud. That's my answer. That's my sign from God. You believe what you want. I believe rain is on the way."

Soon the whole sky turned black. Thunder rolled. Rain fell in sheets all across the barren land. Elijah sat under the tent flap chewing a piece of straw and giggling like a little kid. His servant stood out in the field with his arms stretched wide and his tongue stuck out. The rain on his face and the mud between his toes reminded him that little blessings can turn into big blessings in the hands of a great God.

Do not despise these small beginnings, for the Lord
rejoices to see the work begin.
(Zechariah 4:10 NLT)

FORTY-FIVE

No Ordinary Place

I know of a place where a rustic old bridge crosses a muddy little creek in a thicket of tall pines. As a seventeen-year-old boy, I walked that trail with a sixteen-year-old girl on a brisk fall day. Leaves crunched beneath our feet, and sunshine peeked through half naked trees. I stood on that bridge, looked her in the eye, and wondered—Is this what falling in love feels like?

I know of another place where spotlights hang on spotless walls, where doctors scrub and mothers scream. It's a sterile place where sons are born and daughters see the light of life outside a womb they've always known as home. I stood in that place beside my wife and watched the wonder of all wonders. A tiny life with timeless love looked up at me with trusting eyes as I wondered—Is this what fatherhood feels like?

I know of another place where well-manicured grass and stately old trees grow beside a lazy blue pond. Wild geese bask on sundrenched banks and wait for crumbs of bread beneath droopy weeping willows. Behind them, near a crop of bushes, lies a row of headstones bearing the family name. I stand there with hands in my pockets and questions in my mind wondering—Is this what grief feels like?

I know of yet another place with blue carpet on the floor and a single lightbulb overhead. It's a place with bifold doors, belts, shoes, gloves, and boots; not just a closet, but a prayer closet. And when the light goes off and my head goes down, this common place becomes an uncommon place. The secular morphs into the sacred. The brush of shirts and sweaters feels like angels' wings, and in the mystery of the dark, I sense a familiar hush of glory, and wonder, Is this what God's presence feels like?

What does it take for a simple place to become special, for the mundane to become miraculous, or for the ordinary to become extraordinary? I don't know, but it's happened many times and it'll happen again.

When a hole in the wall with a manger full of hay becomes a place where the Ancient of Days coos and cries, something beyond the norm is going on.

When a Galilean's boat with an empty net becomes a pulpit for the Lion of the tribe of Judah, something special is in the air.

When a brown bag lunch with boney fish and bite-size bread is blessed and broken and multiplied and when thousands are fed by the hands of One whose name is called the Bread of Life, something extraordinary is taking place.

When a rugged tree on a windswept hill stands in the dark in the middle of the day, when the sun shuts its eye and the moon covers its face, when black clouds crawl through shadowed skies at three in the afternoon, and when rocks rumble, graves burst, and veils rip, something heavenly has happened on earth.

When stalwart soldiers faint, when angelic messengers appear, when a heavy stone with a Roman seal rolls aside and frightened disciples with fearful questions run inside, and when he who was dead comes to life and walks among doubters who believe— something marvelous has invaded the mundane.

Today is no ordinary day. This is no ordinary place. God has chosen to reveal himself to you in ways common and uncommon. His wink or prod and his nudge or nod are meant to get your attention. "But this is just a normal day," you say. "There's nothing special about this place." Close your eyes and take a breath. The God who cannot hide is waiting to be found, and he won't be satisfied until you say, "Aha!"

---

*I will be found by you, says the L*ORD.
(JEREMIAH 29:14)

FORTY-SIX

The Jordan River

We were escorted by Israeli military with machine guns mounted on their jeeps. A trail of dust kicked up behind the convoy as we headed to a remote spot in the south, a spot where Jesus once stood. It's a restricted area now, a hot bed of political tension. Usually forbidden to tourists, we were granted special permission to visit for a few minutes. The sun blazed high in the open sky as we arrived at the well-guarded destination.

"Do not get in the water!" the Israeli escort said, without the courtesy of a smile. "The soldiers on the other side of the river have the right to shoot anyone who gets in the water!"

The instructions were loud and clear, and he wasn't joking. We exited the bus with mixed emotions, excitement laced with trepidation. I glanced across the river and counted the armed soldiers eyeing us with guarded interest.

"Let's take a few pictures and get out of here," I thought to myself. "The last thing I want is for my family back home to hear a news flash—Bald Preacher Shot in the Noggin in the Negev or Dead Evangelist Floats to the Dead Sea in a Baptism of Blood."

A small group of us stood on the west side of the river. Jordanian soldiers stood on the east side. We had cameras. They had rifles. Believe me when I say, "No one got in the water." (If you want to be baptized in the Jordan River, you can, but not down south. Baptisms these days take place at a friendlier place up north.)

So this is the spot, huh? This is where Jesus stood waist deep in the Jordan, where he was baptized at the beginning of his ministry. I took a picture upstream and another picture downstream. Then I looked up in the azure sky and took a picture straight overhead. This is where it happened, where the holy dove descended from an open heaven. This is the place of the inauguration of the greatest ministry of all time.

I closed my eyes and tried to imagine the crowd that day. They were eyewitnesses of Christ's ordination, and there wasn't a camera among them. His wet hair clung to his head and shoulders. His robe dripped with river water. His feet left soaked footprints on the bank. His life left a trail of evidence of his holy baptism.

The Spirit led him to the nearby wilderness, inhabited by no one, for no one could survive it. He fasted forty days, fighting hunger by day and demons by night. But the newly baptized Savior emerged victorious in his bout with Beelzebub. He overcame the enemy by the power of the Spirit, the same Spirit that fell on him during his baptism.

Sometime later, religious leaders questioned his authority to teach in the Jerusalem Temple (Mark 11:28). He pointed to the moment of his baptism, the moment of his ministerial ordination. He was rejected by the scribes and Pharisees but was approved by the One who matters most. "This is My beloved Son, in whom I am well pleased" (Matthew 3:17).

I want to remind you, as a Spirit-filled believer, you have divine power and heavenly authority. The Bible says, "You will receive power when the Holy Spirit comes on you; and you will be my witnesses" (Acts 1:8 NIV).

Friend, when you receive the Spirit, you get more than a sensation, more than goosebumps or chills. You get heaven's authority to be Christ's witness on the earth. Don't walk around defeated and forlorn. Remember who you are. You are the blood bought, Spirit taught, faith wrought child of the Most High God. Square your shoulders and lift your chin. God has given you his Spirit on purpose, so live life on purpose.

Keep in mind, the dove that descended upon Jesus also descended upon you. He leads you, guides you, comforts you, and empowers you. Leave a trail of evidence wherever you go.

It is the Spirit who gives life; the flesh profits nothing.
(JOHN 6:63)

The Fig Tree

A fig tree is not just a fig tree. If you're Jewish, it's a lot more than that. It's a place for poached eggs and hot coffee in the morning, a place for warm cookies and cold milk in the evening.

Americans have replaced the fig tree with a front porch, but it serves the same purpose. Whether you prefer a four-legged chair or a bentwood rocker, there's no better place than a front porch to sit a spell and count fireflies on a midsummer's night.

Nathanael had such a place in Cana of Galilee. His lovely home was surrounded by wild iris, date palms, and one very fine fig tree. Twenty paces from the kitchen, it was just far enough for privacy and just close enough for another cake of raisins or a plug of cheese. He and his wife enjoyed ending their day under the fig branches, talking about nothing, like it was everything in the world.

One day Nathanael and his best friend, Philip, sat under the fig tree and discussed the Sabbath Day lesson: deceitful Jacob and his dream of a heavenly ladder. Nathanael insisted, "Because Jacob was deceitful, God revealed himself to him in order to shake him up, to provoke his heart to righteousness."

Philip disagreed, "God reveals himself to all people, the just and the unjust alike. Even pious folks like you, my friend, need their hearts stirred from time to time. And as you think on that, I have to go. I told the wife I'd be home before lunch."

Soon after, Nathanael stood up, stretched, and turned to walk to the house. His wife was cooking fish for lunch, and the smell was irresistible. BAM, out of nowhere, a bolt of lightning hit the top of the fig tree, splitting it like the Red Sea. At that very instant, Nathanael saw the eye of God staring at him from the open sky. He ran to the house in a panic, snatched the door open, and asked his wife, "Did you hear that loud crack of thunder and lightning? It split the top of our fig tree."

"What?" She stepped outside and came back quickly. "You

must be seeing things. The fig tree is fine. It looks just like it did this morning."

"No. The branches parted, and the wind blew, and . . ."

She sighed with disbelief. "Sit down and have some lunch. Your sugar level must have dropped."

As they were finishing lunch, Philip pushed through the front door without knocking. "We found the Messiah." He took a deep breath. "It's Jesus of Nazareth."

Nathanael wrinkled his nose and thought, *Nazareth?* Then he said, "Can anything good come out of Nazareth?" (John 1:46).

"He's on the other side of town. Come see for yourself."

Nathanael wiped his mouth, kissed his wife goodbye, and followed Philip out of the house. When they arrived, Peter and Andrew were sitting on the well. James and John were looking for a rope and a bucket. And Jesus was eating a handful of grapes. "Ah. A true Israelite," Jesus said. "This is a man in whom there is no deceit."

Nathanael was suspicious. How could anyone from small town Nazareth know such things? "We've never met. How do you know me?"

Jesus stepped close and peered into his soul. "We met . . . under your fig tree. It was me. I saw you."

Nathanael dropped to his knees. "Rabbi, you are the Son of God" (John 1:49 NIV).

"Because I said to you, 'I saw you under the fig tree,' do you believe? You will see greater things than these. . . . You shall see heaven open, and the angels of God ascending and descending upon the Son of Man" (John 1:50-51).

Philip helped Nathanael to his feet and whispered in his ear, "Jesus is the ladder in Jacob's dream; he's the mediator between heaven and earth, between God and sinners."

"Yes. I see that now, but how will we ever convince others?"

"Don't worry. As long as there are fig trees (and front porches), God will find a way to speak to those who listen."

Then Jacob awoke from his sleep and said,
"Surely the LORD is in this place."
(GENESIS 28:16)

FORTY-EIGHT

The Court of Gentiles

Jesus squeezed between a lamb and a goat, nodded at an Ethiopian and a Syrian, bumped into a vendor's cart, and stepped over a pile of manure. Twelve perturbed disciples followed right behind him, weaving in and out of the chaotic crowd at the Temple.

The Sanhedrin had just passed a new law allowing merchants to move their booths off of the streets and set up shop in the Court of Gentiles. Tables and tents popped up everywhere. It looked like a full-blown carnival. Clerks exchanged coins, vendors bartered deals, and local peddlers hawked their wares. The only thing missing was a guy walking around with an apron around his neck shouting, "Hot dogs. Get your hot dogs here."

One chatty shopkeeper looked up from his bazaar booth to barter with Jesus. "Two pigeons, sir? How about four? Do you prefer a necklace? We have all kinds. Ah, I know what you need. New sandals. Right? I've got your size right here."

Jesus bent over, picked up a length of rope, and tied a knot in one end. It matched the lump in his throat. Holy fire danced in his eyes. For a moment, he looked more like a street fighter than the Savior. Biceps bulged. Nostrils flared. Veins pulsed.

"Are you alright?" Peter asked. "Your face looks red and—"

"Back up," Jesus snapped.

"Huh?" Before Peter could duck, Jesus grabbed the corner of the table and heaved it in the air. Coins scattered everywhere. Bird cages broke open and doves soared over the eastern gate.

"You've turned my father's house into a marketplace," (Matthew 21:13, author's paraphrase) Jesus scolded the violators as he whipped the rope like a Roman gladiator. Pandemonium broke out. Vendors clutched their moneybags and headed for the hills. Spooked sheep stampeded the nearest exit.

"[This is a] house of prayer for all nations," (Mark 11:17) he reminded them in no uncertain terms.

Once the dust settled, the only people left in the Court of Gentiles were the Gentiles. They clapped their hands in celebration. Their hero had showed up and stood up for their rights.

The Jews were content with a carnival on the holy campus as long as it was limited to the Court of Gentiles. That meant less room for scoundrels and scallywags. The priests and Levites had their place to worship. Jewish men and women had their place to worship. The only group left out were the Gentiles, which was just fine with the self-righteous Sadducees and the sanctimonious Pharisees.

When Gentiles arrived at Jerusalem to worship, they found their place had been confiscated by the carnal-minded and the money hungry. That's why Jesus went ballistic. He fought for the right of all people to worship at the Temple.

If anyone among them knew what it felt like to be left out, Jesus did. He was born in a stable because there was no room in the inn. He was called a madman by his own family. He was run out of town in his old stomping ground, Nazareth. He was kicked to the curb in Gadara. That's why he fought for the Gentiles. So they'd have a valid place of worship.

Are you a Gentile? So am I, from the top of my bald head to the bottom of my bare feet. We may not belong in the twelve tribes of Israel, but we do belong in the family of God. We're not outsiders. We've been grafted in. We are welcome at the foot of the cross, we belong in the blood-bought Church, and we are welcome inside the pearly gates. Why? Because Jesus fought for our rights.

You're not relegated to the back of the line. You're not a second-rate citizen in the kingdom of God. You're a king's kid; a bona fide, card-carrying member of the celestial family. Mount Calvary is your birthplace. Heaven is your final destination.

So if anyone asks you how you got in the family of faith, send them to the man with fire in his eyes and a whip in his hand. He'll set the story straight. When all the finger-pointing stops, you'll be right where you belong—beside Jesus in the house of God.

My house shall be called a house of prayer for all nations.
(ISAIAH 56:7)

FORTY-NINE

The Old Home Place

The house used to be blue. It's a dull gray now, and the rose bush that was under the window is gone. A big oak tree once shaded the front yard where we played as children. My knees were dirty and my shoes untied, but I didn't have a worry in the world. The summer days were warm and long, and life was full of make-believe.

Someone else occupies that old house now, but my memories still live there too—a yellow bike with a banana seat, a dog named Bosley wagging his tail, and a wooden fort made of scrap lumber that leaked when it rained. I can still smell a cake baking in the oven and hear the laughter of little boys playing in cardboard boxes. It was a simple life, a good life filled with honeysuckles and fireflies, ice pops and pop tarts, early morning hugs and goodnight kisses.

When the sun went down, we'd kick the can or play hide-and-seek until Mom called us in for dinner. Family devotions always followed. Mom read the Bible and Dad said the prayers. We three boys knelt by the couch and asked God to bless grandpas, grandmas, uncles, and aunts.

We slept under quilts and dreamed the night away, then woke up in the morning ready to live another day. Oh, the memories. Oh, the simplicity.

That was then, this is now. Times have changed. We got older and life got complicated. And once simplicity is lost, it's hard to find again. Responsibilities demand our attention. Careers dominate our time. Leisure gets lost in the busyness of life, and the holy gets consumed in the hoopla.

Somewhere in the middle of all the noise, there is a quiet place, a simple place. Mary found it at the feet of Jesus (Luke 10:39). The psalmist called it "the secret place of the most High" (Psalm 91:1 KJV), and Jesus referred to it as a "closet" of prayer (Matthew 6:6 KJV). It's the place where we let go of adult-size problems and trust

God with child-like faith. It's the place where worry ends and worship begins, where weeping during the night becomes joy in the morning (Psalm 30:5).

Richard Foster calls it "finding harmony in a complex world".[1]

Jesus said, "Unless you change and become like little children, you will never enter the kingdom of heaven" (Matthew 18:3 NIV).

With that in mind, let's return to my old house. Look in my old bedroom, just beyond the living room, down the hall on the left. My little brother and I sit side-by-side holding a hairbrush and a drumstick for microphones. We're singing a duet. It's a simple song for chaotic times.

> *Jesus loves me, this I know,*
> *for the Bible tells me so.*
> *Little ones to him belong;*
> *they are weak, but he is strong.*
> (ANNA BARTLETT WARNER)[2]

Simplicity . . . is in Christ.
(2 CORINTHIANS 11:3)

FIFTY

In the Middle of the Road

There's a road no parent should have to walk, the one that leads to the cemetery. Children expect to bury their parents, but the reverse is painfully dreadful. It's unnatural, unnerving, and unbearable for parents to bury their children. Tears of grief may lessen over time, but the unanswered questions never go away.

The widow of Nain had walked that road before (Luke 7:12). Her loving husband had died, and she was left to raise the boy alone. It didn't seem fair, but it was her lot in life. Absent her husband's strength, she learned to do the work of both, which is never easy. At least she had a son at home. He could chop wood and draw a bucket of water. They could eat breakfast together in the morning and watch the stars appear at night. They had each other, and a little consolation is better than none at all.

Then it happened again. Cursed be the day. The boy's voice went silent. His ruddy cheeks turned ashen gray. His little fingers lay motionless by his side. The stillness of his heart broke her heart into a thousand pieces. How could she bear to walk that road again?

The path to the cemetery descended from the town of Nain, slithered down the slopes of Mt. Hermon, and finally arrived at the ancestral tomb in the valley below. Winding this way and that, the narrow path was just wide enough to accommodate the pallbearers and the open coffin. Friends and family marched behind in cadence to the mournful flute. Wails and laments rose and fell in waves of grief. Relatives smote their breast in disbelief and woe.

Then the unexpected happened. A group of travelers occupied the road below. They were headed up to the city of Nain. The two crowds converged at the same spot, and one needed to give way to the other.

The crowds were opposite in every way. One was going to the cemetery; the other was going to the city. One was headed down, while the other was headed up. One, with tearful lamentation; the other, with cheerful celebration. One was accompanied by the Death Angel, and the other was led by the Resurrection and the Life.

The narrow road could not hold them both; someone must give right-of-way. Protocol required the crowd headed up the road to step aside, making room for the funeral procession to continue to the grave. But the Life-Giver doesn't yield to death. When others stepped aside, he stepped up.

Jesus positioned himself right in the middle of the road and drew a line in the dirt with his foot. "This far and no farther." Pallbearers gasped. Flute players gawked. The mother slapped her hand over her mouth, and relatives demanded the funeral director do something about the interruption.

Jesus grabbed the coffin with his hand. That's when death lost its grip. The dead boy sat up. The pallbearers perked up. Flute players changed their tune. Mourners stopped crying and started dancing. Mother and son skipped all the way back to Nain and threw a party late into the night.

That's called a divine interruption. When you're on your way down, Jesus is on his way up. He'll meet you in the middle of your road, the middle of your night, or the middle of your storm. He not only turns weeping into dancing; he turns lamentation into celebration, and pallbearers into partiers.

Jesus doesn't follow protocol. That's why you should expect the unexpected: doctor's reports become praise reports, pink slips become promotions, and closed doors become opened windows.

Instead of planning your next pity party, plan a praise party. And make sure Jesus is right in the middle of it, because no one celebrates life better than the Life-Giver.

I have come that they may have life,
and that they may have it more abundantly.
(JOHN 10:10)

FIFTY-ONE

The Secret Place

Although winds of opposition buffeted him on all sides, his heart remained calm. The stillness in his soul never changed. He had a certain peace on the inside, an inner gyroscope, that kept him from falling apart in the tough times.

You name it, he endured it. Bereavement? Check. His cousin was brutally murdered. Betrayal? Check. His best friend abandoned him when he needed him the most. Falsely accused? Check. He was imprisoned and executed, although he never committed a crime. Physically exhausted, emotionally spent, relationally stressed? Check times three.

He was in his thirties, but you might guess him in his fifties. His life was hard and his challenges were great, but he never gave up. No wind could capsize his faith. No calamity could undermine his courage. No adversity could squelch his joy.

He plowed through peril and pain like an icebreaker in frozen seas. He trudged onward and upward in spite of everything his enemies threw at him.

How did he do it? He knew the secret of the secret place.

Jesus made it his habit to frequent still places: a seaside escape, a mountain top view, or a garden getaway. It was his routine to retire to restful places. He started and ended his days in quiet talks with his Father. Those special places were the bookends that held him together, like praying hands cradled around a stack of books. Remove either bookend and the whole stack collapses.

Whose hands held him together? The hands of his Father, of course, the One he communed with on a regular basis.

Here's a small sample:

"Now when Jesus heard about John, He withdrew from there in a boat to a secluded place" (Matthew 14:13 NASB).

"After He had sent the crowds away, He went up on the mountain by Himself to pray; and when it was evening, He was there alone" (Matthew 14:23 NASB).

"Jesus went away from there, and withdrew into the region of Tyre and Sidon" (Matthew 15:21 NASB).

"Departing from there, Jesus went along the Sea of Galilee, and after going up on the mountain, He was sitting there" (Matthew 15:29 NASB).

"And sending away the crowds, Jesus got into the boat and came to the region of Magadan" (Matthew 15:39 NASB).

"And He left them and went away" (Matthew 16:4 NASB).

Here is the secret to Christ's inner peace: alone time with his Father, solitude in a closet of prayer, quiet time in a quiet place. It's the vital secret to catching your breath when you're out of breath.

If we don't "come apart" for private prayer, we will soon come apart at the seams.

Where is your quiet place? The chair by the window? The tree swing? The deer stand? The flower garden? It doesn't always have to be the same place, but it needs to be some place. For me, it's a parked car under a shade tree, a lighted fish aquarium in a dark room, or an empty church on a rainy afternoon.

The only way we can offer peace to a troubled world is to first secure peace in our own heart.

Be still, and know that I am God.
(PSALM 46:10)

FIFTY-TWO

The Coffee Shop

As soon as I walked through the door, I knew I'd found a home away from home. My chilled bones and my somber mood had found a place to comfort one another. The quaint coffee shop, concealed under a cappuccino-colored awning, sat cleverly on the corner of Out of Sight and Out of Mind. After taking two steps inside, I stopped dead in my tracks. It was a slice of paradise, the brewed awakening I'd been waiting for. I determined to make this place my morning oasis for as long as I was in town.

The bossa nova jazz massaged the stress out of my neck and shoulders. The aroma of full-bodied coffee transported me to a place with no time and no trouble. "What will it be today?" the barrister asked, predicting correctly that I'd be back again tomorrow.

"A large vanilla chai with a shot of black coffee."

"Pick a seat," he said. "I'll bring it to you when it's ready."

I chose a leather chair by the window so I could listen to the rain pound the pavement. I silenced my cell phone and laid it face down on the table. This was no time for interruptions. It was "me" time. I closed my eyes and blew out a sigh. When I opened my eyes, my chai had magically appeared, steaming in a heavy burgundy mug.

"I love this place," I whispered to the vacant chair on my left.

BAM. SLAM. The door opened and shut. Two ladies with purses the size of suitcases and voices like megaphones turned Paradise into Gehenna in three seconds flat. It was time for intercession. "Dear God, make those ladies place orders to go so I can sit here and read my Bible in peace and quiet." God didn't answer my prayer. He had better plans.

They complained every breath. The rain had ruined their day, their hair was frizzy, their shoes were soaked, their favorite boutique was closed, the salesman wouldn't honor their coupon—on and on, nonstop.

Tragedy of all tragedies, they plopped down at the table beside me. My eyes widened to saucers. The steam pulsing from my ears matched the steam rising from my cup of Joe. Perhaps I'll swap my mug for a Styrofoam cup and enjoy my latte in the car. I'm not going to let these ladies ruin a perfectly good Monday morning.

"He's the preacher. Ask him," one lady said to the other.

I pretended to smile. "Have we met?"

"You preached at my church yesterday."

"Oh. I don't remember seeing you. I'm sorry," I tried to cover up my covert intentions. Whether we'd met or not, I was headed to the car.

Then the other lady looked at me with sorrow in her eyes. "Why won't God give me a baby?"

My mug was too hot to hold, so I set it down on the edge of their table. "What do you mean?"

The first lady interrupted, "She just got another D&C, her third in three years."

I grabbed an empty chair from the adjacent table and swiveled it around. Now three of us sat at a table for two. "I know how you feel. My wife and I went through the same thing."

"I don't understand," she said. "I thought God loved me. He must hate me."

"I don't know everything about God, but I can tell you this: God loves you no matter what. Besides, there's still hope for you in the future. One of my friends lost eight babies before giving birth to the ninth. That little miracle baby is in med school now, studying to be a doctor. So don't you dare give up on what God can do."

She pulled a wrinkled tissue from her purse and patted her face dry. "Thank you. I feel better now."

"You ladies enjoy the rest of your day." I returned the chair to its proper place, exchanged my mug for a to-go cup, and sat in my car sipping a not-so-hot vanilla chai. Then the Lord reminded me: Life isn't about living in my little corner of paradise. It's about serving slices of paradise to hurting people."

Do not use your freedom to indulge the flesh;
rather, serve one another humbly in love.
(GALATIANS 5:13 NIV)

FIFTY-THREE

The Stormy Sea

Dark clouds swirled overhead like prizefighters stalking each other in the ring. Hot air from the tropics swung first, a sharp uppercut from sea level. Cool breeze retaliated from the mountains, a booming left hook from two thousand feet above. West side waters clashed with east side vapors in the battle of the ages. The slugfest took place on the Sea of Galilee. The spectators were twelve frightened disciples caught right in the middle of the brawl. They clung to their little boat, desperately missing their Captain. He watched from ringside.

Eyewitnesses retold the story in descriptive horror. Matthew said they were "Battered by the waves" (Matthew 14:24 NASB). Mark said they were "straining at the oars" (Mark 6:48 NASB). John added, "the sea grew very rough" (John 6:18 NLT).

Battered? Straining? Rough? Sounds familiar, doesn't it? Could their storm be your storm? Violent winds, stormy seas, and swelling waves. That's a triplet of trouble. *So is* scared stiff, life-threatening, and panic-stricken. What's missing in this story?

Jesus. Jesus is missing. Where is Jesus in this storm? Waves are in my boat, but where's my Master? Wind howls in my ear, but where's his voice? Panic is present, but the Peacemaker is absent.

The disciples might have expected a cold shoulder from Jesus if they had disobeyed his command. But when he said "Get in the boat," they climbed aboard. He said, "Launch forth," and they pushed away from shore. He said, "Sail to the other side," and they hoisted the mainsail. He said it. They did it. That should entitle them to a storm-free voyage, right? Wrong.

Jesus ordered them to sail straight into the teeth of danger, knowing the storm was on its way. He could have warned them about the weather, but he didn't. He could have delayed their trip, but he didn't. He could have sailed with them, but he chose not to.

He deliberately sent them into harm's way. Then he went to the mountaintop to pray. He prayed for their courage. He interceded for their faith. He watched for their tipping point. And when he knew the time was right, he walked to them on the water.

It took them hours to row to the middle of the lake. It took him only minutes. Why? Because the wind that hindered them didn't hinder him. He strolled on the waves they struggled with.

In two thousand years, he hasn't changed one bit. When you feel abandoned, he's still watching. When you feel panicked, he's still praying.

Your storm won't sink you; it will only strengthen you. It's not your comfort he's after, it's your character. He wants you to become more like him, storm tested and father approved.

We know that all things work together for good
to those who love God, to those who are the called
according to His purpose.
(ROMANS 8:28)

FIFTY-FOUR

The Tree Swing

*T*he neighbor's fence was just the right height to stand on while leaning back in the seat of the tree swing. At eleven years old, this was the location of my Olympic "rope gymnastics" tournaments. With just the right propulsion, I could perform backward flips, double turns, and spin-a-roos while landing perfectly on both feet in the grass. (Well, "perfectly" is a matter of opinion, but since I was the only judge, perfection was always the outcome.)

The man who lived there didn't approve of us kids standing on his fence rail, so the tournament always took place while he was at work. If he only had a little more appreciation for world class tree swinging, he would have set up concession stands and judges' booths with score cards. But grumpy adults are usually too busy to see the hidden talents and lofty dreams of dirty-faced kids.

When the coast was clear, I leaped over the back fence and trotted down the alley to the neighbor's yard, climbed over his fence, and assumed the starting position in the tree swing. Not a soul was there to watch the historic event. My only witness was the gray squirrel with a cheek full of acorns and the stray cat hiding under the shed.

I imagined hearing the roar of the crowd. Trumpets sounded the commencement of the Backyard Games. Contestants shivered in their shoes, knowing that Clifton Jay was on the docket and predicted to win *first place*, just as he had done a hundred times before.

"Ladies and Gentlemen, the day has arrived, the moment we've all been waiting for. In this final event, the winner will be crowned as the undisputed champion of Olympic tree swinging. Turn your eyes and tune your ears. This is the chance of a lifetime."

Standing on the fence rail, with my bottom sitting snuggly in the rubber seat, I nodded to the crowd as a courtesy and began my double-turn, knee-tuck, toe-extension, and backflip, this time with my eyes closed. Leaping from the swing on the far end, I landed on both feet, raised both arms in the air, and lifted my chin to the sky. The roar of the crowd was deafening. The applause continued with a standing ovation. They begged for more.

"Ladies and Gentlemen, believe it or not, Clifton Jay has decided to return to the swing one more time. By public demand and in unprecedented fashion, you will get to see the amazing feat yet again, at no extra charge."

"Hey, you! I thought I told you to stop climbing on my fence!" The grumpy old man was home from work. The Olympics would have to wait until another day.

"Pretend" approval was squashed by "real" disapproval in a matter of seconds. That's the way life goes, right? Children want approval from their parents. Wives want approval from their husbands. Employees want approval from their bosses. It's a never-ending rat race. It seems no matter how hard we try, we always come up short.

Disapproval is a lifelong companion. Eventually, we feel like we can't please anyone anymore, including God.

Lofty goals are forgotten, and childhood dreams are abandoned. We beat ourselves up with condemnation and ridicule. "I'm nobody. I can't do anything right. I'm a failure. Why even try?"

I want to remind you that you were created in the image of God, and he don't "make no junk." You are a masterpiece, a winner, an overcomer; dare I say, you are a gold medal winner in God's eyes.

The Bible says in Jude 1:24 that God is "able to keep you from falling, and to present you faultless before the presence of his glory" (KJV). Faultless? That means on Judgment Day, if your faith is in Christ alone, you will finally hear the approval you've always craved, "Well done, my good and faithful servant. . . . Let's celebrate together!" (Matthew 25:21 NLT).

But you don't have to wait until then. You're the apple of God's eye right now. So go ahead—do your backflip, double turn, spin-a-roo. The winner's medallion in God's hand is designed to fit around your neck. You're his child and he's proud of you.

Now unto him that is able to keep you from falling,
and to present you faultless before the presence
of his glory with exceeding joy.
(JUDE 1:24 KJV)

FIFTY-FIVE

Mount Hermon

No one climbs Mount Hermon by mistake. It's the destination of the determined. Topped with its signature white snow cap, it towers over the Promised Land like an ancient guardian. Its formidable winds have turned back many well-intended travelers, but Jesus would not give up so easily. Any man who can bear the weight of Mount Calvary can certainly climb the height of Mount Hermon. Besides, what's a little snow to a man who walks on water? Jesus pulled his cloak over his ears and pressed on, one step at a time. He knew full well the glory at the top was worth the grind at the bottom.

Following in his footsteps were three cold-blooded compadres: Peter, James, and John. The higher they climbed, the colder they got. James and John chitchatted along the way, but Peter's mind was elsewhere. He was still miffed about Jesus's rebuke six days earlier. With every huff and puff up the rugged mountain, Peter rehearsed the tongue-lashing from Jesus, "Get behind Me, Satan!" (Matthew 16:23). Of all things to say to a friend, couldn't Jesus have picked a better word? Pal, Bud, Chum, Amigo. Anything would've been better than Satan. Peter was only trying to keep Jesus from suffering on the cross and going to an early grave. What's wrong with that?

Here's what's wrong with that. Instead of taking orders from the Master, Peter assumed the role of the Master and gave orders to Jesus. "Far be it from You, Lord; this shall not happen to You!" (Matthew 16:22).

Peter thought the crucifixion was untimely and inappropriate. It didn't jive with his theology. He believed Christ would overthrow the Roman Empire, liberate Israel from foreign dominance, and set up his kingdom on earth right away. Peter's belief system plugged his ears to any message contrary to his wishes. Although he knew Jesus was the Messiah, he rejected the timing and scope of the Messiah's mission. No wonder Jesus called him Satan; Peter had aligned himself with the Adversary.

To solve the problem, Jesus summoned Peter, James, and John to the summit of Mount Hermon, where their view of present suffering would be balanced by an unobstructed view of future glory.

The zigzag route up the snowy slope rewarded them with breathtaking sights. However, Jesus's plan for the day included much more than scenic overviews. He wanted them to see something they'd remember when overcome with grief about his death. They needed to see the Messiah dressed in Shekinah from head to toe, a once-in-a-lifetime view of heaven on earth.

No one had seen Christ in his full glory, like this, before. His divine majesty had remained hidden beneath his flesh since the day he was born. Oh, a few wedding guests caught a glimpse of it in Cana when he turned water into wine, and a few others sneaked a peek when he multiplied fish and bread to feed the hungry thousands. But no one had ever seen Christ dressed in the full measure of his glory *until now*. And Mount Hermon was the ideal place for the revealing. The midday sun danced on the snow like a ballerina in a field of diamonds. It was the perfect backdrop for heaven's Holy One to prove that suffering in the present can't compare to glory in the future.

When they finally reached the frozen summit, Peter, James, and John collapsed on the ground. But Jesus stood tall, his eyes open, his hands raised. Then it happened. His flesh faded to the background as his spirit stepped to the foreground. Blinding light emanated from his face. His hair glowed celestial white. His regal robe outshined a thousand suns. The last time Jesus looked like this he was in heaven, the day before Mary wrapped him in swaddling clothes.

Angels bowed. Heaven hushed. Earth trembled. And Peter got tongue-tied. That's when the divine Arbiter showed up in a cloud and put Peter in his place. "This is My beloved Son, in whom I am well pleased. Hear Him!" (Matthew 17:5).

Thus the lesson of Mount Hermon's adventure comes into focus: When your plans don't line up with God's plans, stop talking long enough to listen to Jesus. And if suffering is a part of today's plan, it's only because Shekinah is on the calendar for tomorrow.

This is My beloved Son, in whom I am well pleased. Hear Him!
(MATTHEW 17:5)

FIFTY-SIX

The Promenade

It's the time of day I love the most. The sun sets behind the western hills, and a grayish haze creeps over the city. Old folks sit on front-porch rockers, and lightening bugs prepare to charm the night. It's the best time for a leisure walk. Take off your sunglasses, take a deep breath, and take a moment to sense the magic of twilight.

This is what I call promenade time. Why?

A few years ago, my family took a vacation to Disney World. One evening, after the sweltering Florida sun finally hid below the horizon, my wife and I walked around the promenade of EPCOT's World Showcase.

There's a gorgeous lagoon in the center of the park, which is surrounded by architectural wonders of the world, from the Eiffel Tower in France to the Temple of Heaven in China, eleven countries in all. You can walk around the world in less than an hour, and the early evening is the magical moment to take it all in.

Tired kids slept in strollers, street-side vendors offered funnel cakes and cappuccinos, and oriental lamps dotted cobblestone walkways.

My wife and I walked a slow cadence. The midday rush was over. Cool evening breezes wafted away our worries, and the first sight of moonlight poured a little romance on the fire. It's a moment captured in my memory that I've relived many, many times. It's a euphoria I long for on days when adult-size problems rob me of child-size joys.

Now every time I sense the magical combination of cool evening breezes with a quiet moment of reflection, my soul whispers, "It's promenade time."

This week, two of my friends breathed their last breath on earth. Then they took their first breath in a place that takes your breath away. They have joined the celestial host of other faithful believers who've gone on before.

The evening breezes blow. The struggles of life are over. The promenade in heaven must be too grand and glorious to describe: mansions fair, glories rare, streets of gold, and saints of old. And the best part is the timeless stroll by the river of life, hand in hand with the Giver of Life. It's an eternity of sacred smiles, joyful laughs, and perfect peace.

Although my heart is broken at the loss of my friends, I'm of a mind to push my tears aside, sit on the front porch, smile toward heaven and whisper, "It's promenade time."

Then the angel showed me the river of the water
of life, as clear as crystal, flowing from the
throne of God and of the Lamb.
(REVELATION 22:1 NIV)

FIFTY-SEVEN

The Emmaus Road

When does seven miles feel like seventy? When someone breaks your heart and steals your hope, just like someone broke the Roman seal and stole the body of Jesus. That's what Cleopas would say if you asked him.

Cleopas who? You remember. He was one of the two disciples sulking on the Emmaus road, the seven-mile road to Jerusalem that turned into a marathon.

"Now behold, two of them were traveling that same day to a village called Emmaus, which was seven miles from Jerusalem" (Luke 24:13). Five verses later, Luke informs us that one of these two disciples was a man named Cleopas.

Look at him walking home. His brow is furrowed, his shoulders are drooped, and his chin is dragging. Someone recently told me that Cleopas is Joseph's brother. If that's true, that means he is the Messiah's uncle. So why is he acting more like a monkey's uncle? Because of all the surprises in his life this past week. His nephew was arrested, although he had committed no crimes. He was falsely judged in a kangaroo court and promptly executed. That was three days ago. This morning Cleopas heard that someone stole his body from the grave. How does Messianic hope on a Friday turn into a train wreck by Sunday? It's as easy as one, two, three—one long road, two sad disciples, and three days since Jesus died.

Cleopas shuffled down the road, mulling over the unsolved mystery: the case of the missing body. Jerusalem lie behind him full of questions. Emmaus, in front of him without an answer. The seven miles in between was littered with dirt kicking and head-scratching.

However, the biggest surprise of all was about to take place. A "stranger" caught up to him along the road and asked, "What are you discussing?" (Luke 24:17 NIV).

Cleopas cocked his head, "You must be the only person in Jerusalem who hasn't heard" (Luke 24:18 NLT).

"Heard what?" Jesus brushed a finger over his mustache to hide a sneaky smile. (If anyone knew what was going on in the city the past few days, he did.) Cleopas didn't realize that the stranger he was talking to was the risen Savior.

He rushed headlong into the sordid facts. "Jesus of Nazareth was a prophet, mighty in word and deed. Our rulers condemned him to die, and the Romans crucified him. Some women went to his tomb and found it empty. They said they saw an angel and that Jesus is alive." The look of chagrin on his face proved he didn't believe the resurrection part of the story. "We had hoped he was the Messiah."

Now the truth comes out. He believed Jesus was the Messiah before he died, before their hopes were dashed. After Jesus died, Cleopas demoted him to prophet (good but not great). He could free a man from blindnesss but not free Israel from Roman oppression.

The stranger (Jesus) had about all he could take of the nonsense, so he retold the story: the brazen serpent, the scapegoat, the show-bread, and the olive branch. He rehearsed the history prophet by prophet, mile after mile. Isaiah's man of sorrows. Daniel's mysterious rock. Hosea's love for Gomer. Then, just as they approached Cleopas's house, he concluded his argument, "And that's why the Messiah had to suffer and die. Are you still reluctant to believe?"

"Stay with us, for it is nearly evening; the day is almost over. So he went in to stay with them" (Luke 24:29 NIV).

They locked the door, lit a candle, and set the table.

"Sir, would you offer grace?" Cleopas asked the stranger.

Jesus took the bread and looked up to Heaven, "Father, provider of all good things, we give thanks." He tore the bread from the top. "For by Your hands we were created." He flipped the bread over and tore it from the bottom. "And by Your hands we are fed. Amen." Then he vanished.

Only Jesus broke bread in such a fashion. When Jesus offered grace at the table, Cleopas realized the stranger was really Jesus.

What's true of Cleopas is true with us. We see Jesus when we receive his grace.

Then their eyes were opened and they knew Him;
and He vanished from their sight.
(LUKE 24:31)

FIFTY-EIGHT

Church Town

When he first strode into town on his white horse, there wasn't much to see. He stopped in the middle of the dusty road, pushed his wide-brimmed hat up a little higher, and took a look around. An empty wagon. An empty trough. An empty porch. Church Town was nearly dried up. Tumbleweed rolled at his feet, and the sun blazed over his shoulder.

He dismounted his horse and got a stack of papers from his leather satchel. He tacked the posters on every building, first on one side of the road, then the other. When he walked through the swinging doors of the cafe, every eye in the place looked at him.

"Howdy, stranger," Sheriff Pete said. "What's your name?"

"JC Peacemaker." He took his hat off and held it in both hands like a gentleman.

"You huntin' some vittles?" said a rancher named Matt.

"No. I'm roundin' up some good men to catch this feller." He held up a Wanted Poster. "Any of you guys seen him?"

"Who's that? And what's he done?" asked Cowboy James, as landowner Phil and Bart listened intently.

"His name is Lu C. Fer. And he's wanted, dead or alive. He's a killer. He's a thief. He ransacks homes and ruins lives. He robs, pillages, and destroys everything he gets his hands on. I intend to hogtie him and throw him in jail for a thousand years."

"That's the feller we was just talkin' 'bout before you walked in here," Andy said. "He's the one who stole our joy."

"Yep," said Pete. "And he's the one who nearly killed my mother-in-law."

"Where's that rascal from anyway?" Tom asked.

"A town called Gehenna, just a stone's throw from Hades. It's in the Badlands. I spent three days there, and I can tell you, it's full of snakes and slime pits."

Cowboy John stood up. "Count me in." He strapped on his holster and twirled his six-shooter 'round his finger. "I'll ride with you, Peacemaker. We gotta stop this guy before he does more harm."

Every Cowboy in the place lined up and swore allegiance. Pete took the badge off of his chest and gave it to Peacemaker.

"There's a new Sheriff in town!'"

JC deputized each volunteer and called them the Apostle Gang. Then they loaded up their rifles and mounted their horses.

"Just a final word of instruction, fellows. As you go, remember you have my authority. 'Heal the sick, cleanse the lepers, raise the dead, cast out demons. Freely you have received, freely give' (Matthew 10:8). Don't slow for swollen rivers. Don't quit in blistering deserts. Blaze the trail before you. Don't worry about what's behind you.

"And one more thing. Pete, leave a note in Church Town for other volunteers to join us. We've got a lot of territory to cover and need all the help we can get. Tell 'em to get revived and join us in Next Town.

"Alright boys, hitch 'em up. Head 'em out."

"Come on, y'all. Let's go."

"Yee-haw!"

And they went out and preached everywhere,
the Lord working with them and confirming the word
through the accompanying signs.
(MARK 16:20)

FIFTY-NINE

Mars Hill

Looking at his ordinary clothes, you'd never guess he was a brilliant man. His sandals were worn, his cloak was old, and his cincture was frayed at the bottom. It didn't seem to bother him though. His steps were steady and his smile was contagious. He was usually surrounded by a crowd, but he walked alone for a change.

The seaport was bustling with merchants, and the chatter of salesmen flooded the market. But their frenzy didn't faze him one bit. He strolled by the vendors with the leisure of a morning walk, whistling a tune only he could hear.

The gray in his beard bore his age, and the wrinkles on his forehead proved his hardships, but the twinkle in his eye told a different story. In spite of this man's tough life, he was lock in step with irresistible joy.

It was a five-mile walk from the coastline to the city square, which gave him plenty of time to relish the salty air and enjoy the warmth of the Mediterranean sun.

As he approached the ancient city of Athens, his spirit became agitated. Idol gods sprouted from every corner. Marble temples housed man-made deities. Market places sold handheld relics. The city pulsed with paganism. He had to say something. The truth in his heart could not be contained.

In synagogues and on street corners, to Epicureans and Stoics, Paul preached the crucified Savior and the resurrected Lord. Their intrigue led to an invitation. Soon he stood before a council of philosophers at the outcropping known as Mars Hill.

"Dear Athenians, you are indeed a very religious people. Your temples are massive. Your gods are many. Yet among such intellectuals, I observe your ignorance." (Eyebrows furrowed. Egotists bristled.)

"What is this babbler trying to say?" (Acts 17:18 NIV).

Paul beckoned with his hand and continued. "On one of your altars, I saw the inscription: 'To the Unknown God.' He is no longer unknown. I know him. So can you. He can't be sheltered on the earth in marble temples. No. He's the one who shelters you under the heavens. He's not man-made; he made man. You know the saying, 'In him we live. In him we move. In him we breathe.' You don't need to stumble in the dark trying to find him; he's right in front of you, within arm's reach. It's time to rethink your life and reject your assumptions. One day you'll stand before the Judge. You'll have to give an account of your life, not to one of these statues, but to the Savior. 'Which Savior?' you ask. The one God identified when he raised him from the dead. He's credible. He's the Christ."

Some slapped their knees in laughter. Others clapped their hands with approval. Two notable citizens followed Paul home and came to saving faith. One was named Dionysius and the other was Damaris. Paul's mission was accomplished in Athens. He brushed his hands and hit the road.

Times have changed since then, but the truth remains the same. I'm not Paul. You're not Damaris. This is a different place and a different day, but the offer to know God still stands.

How can you know the Unknown God? The same way as always, through his son whom he raised from the dead, Jesus.

Whoever calls on the name of the LORD shall be saved.
(ROMANS 10:13)

SIXTY

The Gazebo

Do you like gazebos as much as I do? I find them instantly attractive. Whether I find one in a front yard or a back lot, on a mountain side or on the shoreline, I'm drawn to gazebos like a magnet. Some have chairs, others have swings. Some are elaborate, others are simple. But they all have one thing in common: they are relaxing. What could be better than a slow rain, a good book, and a quiet gazebo? Sign me up.

My wife and I had a gazebo once. It was short-lived. A snowstorm took it down. The vinyl tore, the screen ripped, and the poles bent. It was irreparable, so we had to throw it away. But it served its purpose while it lasted, and I'm still thankful for it today.

Our gazebo sat in the front yard, on the east side of the house. It sat back in an enclave of pine trees and was surrounded by six tiki lamps on bamboo poles. The lone piece of furniture underneath the canopy was a cushioned bench swing. Fine mesh screening kept the gnats out. It was the perfect place for a cup of morning coffee or a late-night mug of hot chocolate. It was the place my wife and I used to chat at the end of the day. We'd sit side by side on the glider and watch the sunset in the evening sky.

When I look back now, I think the Lord provided that gazebo for us during a special time in our lives. It was the time we needed it the most. I still remember the day like it was yesterday.

I was in Newbern, Virginia, in the home of my close friend. My cell phone rang in the adjacent room. When I answered, it was my wife. She was in tears. I closed the door for a moment of privacy as she told me the doctor's report from MCV in Richmond. They said the test results were not good. That kind of news will turn your world upside down in a hurry.

I headed home right away. It was a long four-hour drive. You can cry a lot of tears in four hours, especially if you think the one you love the most doesn't have long to live. When I pulled up in the driveway, I ran from the car to the house to get to my wife as quickly as possible. But with peripheral vision, I saw she was in the gazebo. That was the perfect place to deal with our imperfect life. I walked across the yard and joined her under the gazebo. We hugged. We cried. We prayed. We questioned. And then we sat side by side on the glider and held on to each other for dear life.

Over the next few weeks, that gazebo became our prayer place, our solace in the storm, and our cleft in the rock. It was the place of peace in our chaotic world. God provided it for us, "for *such* a time as this" (Esther 4:14).

Thank God our story has a good ending. The next series of tests came back negative. She was given a clean bill of health, and I thank God for it every day.

A few winters later a snowstorm ruined our gazebo. But that's okay. It had already served its purpose. It was our green pastures, still waters, and the place where God restored our soul (Psalm 23:2-3).

I share this lesson with you to remind you that God knows exactly what you need and when you need it. You might not need last year's gazebo this year, but whatever you do need, he will provide it. The God of gazebos is your heavenly Father, and his grace is never in short supply.

Your Father knows exactly what you need.
(MATTHEW 6:8 NLT)

PART THREE

Purpose to Fulfill

SIXTY-ONE

I Love You This Much

Do you remember what it feels like to fall in love? The nervous jitters and the silly willies? You know what I mean? The sweaty palms, the stammers, the shakes, and the skipped heartbeats?

Falling in love is one of the "funniest" things you'll ever do. There's no guarantee you won't lose a few hairs, a few marbles, or a few nights' sleep before it's over. It should come with a warning label. It'll make you do the craziest things, like talk on the phone for four hours straight or write a love letter eighteen pages long or drive fourteen hours nonstop just to say hello (and get a kiss). I not only have the T-shirt, I own the wardrobe.

When I was twenty years old, I was engaged and in love. That was back in the day when I had hair on my head instead of in my ears. My waist was thin, my smile was wide, and my eyes were glossy. I was working in southern Mississippi, but my fiancé was in central Virginia. We had no cellphones, no Facebook, no Instagram, no Twitter, and no email. All we had was snail mail. What's that? Lick a stamp, pray a prayer, and hope it gets there before you do. (Don't knock it. Puppy love was here before the Pony Express.)

My work week was over on Friday, and I was headed home on Saturday. It was a thousand-mile trip, but love counts by the minute not by the mile. "If I eat lunch at a drive-through instead of a sit-down, I can see her in thirteen hours."

My journey started early in the morning. I hoped to make it to Bristol, Tennessee, by midafternoon. If so, that'd give me a gambler's chance of seeing my girl before midnight. (Cupid shot me with two arrows: one in my heart and the other in my lead foot.)

I rolled the window down, cranked up the radio, and hit the road like Wile E. Coyote chasing the Road Runner. When I passed the Bristol exits, I never pumped the brakes. When Radford was in my rearview mirror, Roanoke was just over the next hill. When

Lynchburg disappeared behind the horizon, Petersburg was just a stone's throw away. What's a thousand miles to a man in love? Nothing but a spin around the block.

Reason says: "Take it slow. Find a motel. Get a good night's sleep. You can see Angie sometime tomorrow."

But I say, "I'm going to see that girl tonight if it hair lips the Pope."

I'd swim the deepest ocean and scale the tallest mountain. I'd lasso the moon and hogtie the sun. I'd crawl through broken glass and wade through a river of alligators. Why? Because love doesn't see the obstacle; it only sees the object of its passion.

Rebecca loved Isaac enough to wave goodbye to her family and leave her childhood home. Jacob loved Rachel enough to work fourteen years for the right to marry her.

Jesus loved you enough to abandon heaven so he could live with you on earth. He exchanged angels and saints for demons and sinners. He discarded regal robes for swaddling clothes and vacated a throne for a manger. Why? Because he loves you.

He gave his hands to the nails, his head to the thorns, his back to the whip, and his life on the cross. How much does he love you? Ask him. He'll stretch his arms wide and say, "I love you this much."

He loves you to the grave and back. And no one but Jesus loves like that.

"Yes, I have loved you with an everlasting love."
(JEREMIAH 31:3)

SIXTY-TWO

Get Up

He stirred a stick in dying embers and sat alone in the dark of night, the night he'd hoped would never come. Only a sliver of moonlight winked over the crest of Mount Hebron. The empty chair on his left and the empty hole in his heart reminded him that the one he loved the most was gone. Their time together had ended too quickly.

It seemed but yesterday that they fell in love. Her skin was soft as silk, her voice sounded like angels, and her beauty was unmatched throughout the land. They etched their names in the bark of a tree and held each other closely in the autumn chill. He kissed her in the evening light and promised to love her forever.

But now she's gone, and he's right back where he started, alone. His mind raced through a thousand memories, but none of them had the power to bring her back. Sarah lay in the dark in the Cave of Machpelah. Abraham sat in the dark in the plains of Mamre. Then he did what he'd always done. He tossed his stick in the ashen coals and got up.

It's the same thing he did every time he got down—he got up again. It was his survival tactic. "Then Abraham [got] up" (Genesis 23:3). That's how he made it through the day, and that's how he made it through the night.

"Abram, get up." That's how God started the conversation when he wanted Abram to leave his hometown of Ur and move his family to a place far away (see Genesis 12:1). So Abram got up and started packing. When God told him to sacrifice his beloved son Isaac on the mountains of Moriah, Abraham got up and saddled the donkey. When an army attacked Sodom and captured his nephew Lot, Abraham got up and pursued them. And when Sarah died and was buried in the cave of Machpelah, Abraham got up again.

Getting up once is never enough, because you get down more

than that. It's a repeated action needed at a time of inaction. It's what you do when you don't know what to do. It's how you live when you feel like dying. It's how you press on when you feel like quitting. You get up.

It's what you do after the divorce and after the surgery. It's what you do after the layoff and after the put-down. It's what you do after the rejection and after the ridicule.

What did Jesus do when he heard the cry of a demon-possessed man in the hills of Gadara? He got up and crossed the lake. He got up and made a difference. What did Jesus do when he saw the disciples straining at the oars in the storm on the lake? He got up and walked on water. He got up and reminded them he was there.

And what did Jesus do when he was wrapped in grave clothes and buried in a cave? What did he do when the Romans sealed the tomb? What did he do when Caiaphas gloated, when Herod laughed, and when Satan celebrated? Jesus did what he always does. He got up.

So can you.

And now what are you waiting for? Get up.
(ACTS 22:16 NIV)

SIXTY-THREE

Ten Seconds of Courage

Hollywood's best movies have nothing on the real-life dramas of the Bible. From romance to murder, from political schemes to public betrayals, the Bible is chock-full of riveting stories. Even critics have to agree, the plots and subplots of biblical narrative are out of this world.

One of the most intriguing stories in the Bible pits a common shepherd boy against a colossal giant: David versus Goliath.

Look at the tale of the tape. Goliath is a man of war, with medals on his chest. David is a runny-nose kid, with sheep dung on his sandals. Goliath has grit. David has pimples. Goliath has abs made of steel. David has ribs made of toothpicks. Goliath weighs seven hundred pounds. David weighs all of ninety-eight pounds, soaking wet. Goliath can dunk a basketball on his knees. David might dunk it with a ten-foot ladder.

Vegas odds say David doesn't have a chance. But we know better, don't we? Because it has nothing to do with David's stature. It has everything to do with David's God.

Goliath's god is a half-man, half-fish god, a carved idol named Dagon. He stands on a rock pedestal in the temple of Gaza. But David's God doesn't live in man-made temples. He reigns in heaven, rules the universe, and flings galaxies into existence.

Goliath's god has eyes, but he can't see; ears, but he can't hear; and hands, but he can't help. David's God watches over every living thing. He feeds the sparrows in the morning and the owls in the evening. He stretches his legs across the Milky Way and props his feet up on a stool called earth (Matthew 5:35).

Look at Goliath standing in the Valley of Elah. He's the perfect blend of Andre the Giant and Blackbeard, the pirate. His muscles bulge, his veins pulse, and his breath stinks. Nothing scares this guy. His voice sounds like thunder, and his legs look like cedars.

Now look at David. You'll need a magnifying glass to get a

good look. (That's a reference to the movie *Honey, I Shrunk the Kids*.) Little David stands on an anthill to make himself a wee bit taller. He has a slingshot in his right hand and a fistful of rocks in his left pocket. He doesn't look like much, does he? Not with that peach fuzz on his chin and those freckles on his face. But just wait.

"Goliath walked out toward David with his shield bearer ahead of him, sneering in contempt at this ruddy-faced boy. 'Am I a dog,' he roared at David, 'that you come at me with a stick?' And he cursed David by the names of his gods" (1 Samuel 17:41-43 NLT). That's the old Philistine version of "Fee, fi, fo, fum!" But it didn't intimidate David one bit.

While Goliath belched out blasphemies, David rolled up his sleeves and determined to make good on a promise he'd made to King Saul. "The LORD who rescued me from the claws of the lion and the bear will rescue me from this Philistine!" (1 Samuel 17:37 NLT).

This was David's bullhorn moment. (Perhaps you remember when President Bush stood atop the wreckage of the Twin Towers with a bullhorn, three days after the terrorists knocked them down.)

David shouted, "You come to me with sword, spear, and javelin, but I come to you in the name of the LORD" (1 Samuel 17:45 NLT). As if that wasn't enough, he added, "The whole world will know that there is a God in Israel!" (President Bush would be proud.)

David whirled that rock overhead in his sling. Like a propeller on a helicopter, around and around it went. Then ZAP—it sailed through the air like it was shot out of a cannon. ZING—it hit Goliath right between the eyes. The giant hit the dirt with a thud, and the shepherd boy secured his place in the annals of history.

All it took was ten seconds of courage. That's right. Ten seconds of courage overcame forty days of intimidation and set the nation free. It still works today.

Lift your chin. Square your shoulders. Take a deep breath. Now count to ten and see what God can do.

So David triumphed over the Philistine
with only a sling and a stone.
(1 SAMUEL 17:50 NLT)

SIXTY-FOUR

Jalopies for Jesus

He pushed his heavy glasses up by the bridge and faked a smile. "Well, how much?" I asked. He scribbled a number on a small piece of paper, turned it upside down, and slid it across the table. I was already nervous, but his sheepish grin and furtive gestures made me feel worse.

No wonder used car salesmen get such a bad rap. This guy fit the stereotype to a T, or I should say to an S: sly, sneaky, and slippery as a snake. Trading cars is at the bottom of my want-to list. I'd rather slide down a sliding board of razors in a thin pair of . . . Well, you get the point.

I knew my old jalopy wasn't worth much, but I was expecting a fair shake. I had my eye on the beauty in the car lot, the one with the shiny wax job, the new leather smell, and the hood wide open. The power on the inside matched the pizzazz on the outside.

Balloons were waving, confetti was falling, and I was dreaming—all signs of a good day. I could see myself in my new ride: windows down, music up, and hair blowing in the breeze. (Wait a minute. I don't have any hair to blow in the breeze, and I haven't bought the car yet.)

I picked up the note he'd slid across the table to me and turned it over. My heart sank. My dream turned into a nightmare. "That's all?" I said. The trade-in value was dirt in a world of diamonds. "That's the number the boss gave me," he shrugged as he pulled a piece of broken toothpick out of his front teeth.

I shuffled back to my old car and drove home in silence. (Correction: It was not in silence. I drove home listening to squeaky brakes, whiny power steering, and the putt-putt-poof of the muffler.)

The lesson of the day: You can't trade if you don't have something valuable to offer.

That's why I had such a hard time grasping the truth of the

gospel. The preacher said, "Come as you are. Bring your faults and failures. Come to Jesus and he'll give you eternal life." The soloist sang:

> *Just as I am, without one plea,*
> *but that thy blood was shed for me,*
> *and that thou bidd'st me come to thee,*
> *O Lamb of God, I come.*

"But I have nothing to offer," I thought. "I've lied, stolen, cheated, swindled, cursed, and a host of other things. God doesn't want someone like me."

> *Just as I am, and waiting not*
> *to rid my soul of one dark blot.*
> (CHARLOTTE ELLIOTT)[1]

With nothing to offer but an old jalopy, I made my way to the altar and traded with Jesus. He signed his name in blood and gave me the deal of a lifetime: his righteousness for my unrighteousness, his joy for my misery, his everything for my nothing.

Today, I'm partnering with Jesus in the soul-winning business by spreading the good news: Jesus trades joy for jalopies.

> *"Come now, and let us reason together,"*
> *Says the LORD,*
> *"Though your sins are like scarlet,*
> *They shall be as white as snow."*
> (ISAIAH 1:18)

SIXTY-FIVE

A Case of Mistaken Identity

Several years ago, I left Virginia Beach after an early-morning seminar and set out for home. The traffic was bumper-to-bumper, so I decided to get out of the traffic and get something to eat.

I pulled off at one of the Williamsburg exits and chose a restaurant at random. As soon as I stepped inside, I wondered if I'd made a mistake. Nearly a dozen people were waiting to be seated, and I had quicker options close by.

Just as I turned to leave, the hostess grabbed me by the elbow. "Follow me, sir. We already have your table prepared."

How could that be? I had only decided to eat there moments before. I wanted an explanation, but she was several steps ahead of me, leading the way. I followed her through the main dining hall and into a special room in the back.

As soon as we stepped inside, she closed a heavy curtain for privacy. The place was nearly soundproof. A circular table sat in the middle of the room with a gorgeous bouquet as a centerpiece. She directed me to a leather chair and asked me to be seated.

"Welcome back," she said. "We always look forward to serving you." Then she exited the room.

I knew they had the wrong guy. I'd never been there before. A waitress asked for my beverage of choice.

"Just water. No lemon."

A second waitress asked for my food order.

"Um, I already have a waitress. She took my drink order."

"Sir, both of us are waiting on you today." She smiled and acted like waiting on me was the best part of her day.

They must think I'm a regional manager or some kind of food critic? I cleared my throat and acted like I was a VIP.

"Steak and eggs, please. Medium on the steak, well done on the eggs. Hash browns on the side. Wheat toast unbuttered, a small bowl of fresh fruit, and chilled tomato juice," I said without looking at the menu.

After I was stuffed to the gills, one of the waitresses offered pastries on a double-decked roll cart.

"I'll have the cheese Danish with a cup of coffee, black."

Finally, I asked for my check so I could head home.

"Oh, no sir. You never have to pay when you come here."

I smiled like I'd been there before and thanked her for her service. After leaving a handsome tip on the table, I slipped past the curtain and waddled through the main dining hall.

The chef, with a tall white hat on his head, rushed out of the kitchen and greeted me before I got away. "Sir, was your breakfast cooked to order? Was everything to your liking?"

"Exquisite. It was perfect. Delicious."

He nodded like his next raise depended on it. He escorted me to the door. "Have a nice day, sir, and come back any time."

"I assure you, I will be back."

I sat in my car and laughed. "Whoa! Who do they think I am? And what are they going to do when the real guy shows up?"

Clearly, it was a case of mistaken identity.

My experience that day reminds me of a fellow in the Bible named Mephibosheth (2 Samuel 9:6). Lame in both feet and living in the badlands of Lo-debar, he was introverted, rejected, and hopeless *until* the day King David invited him to the palace in Jerusalem. From that day forward, for the rest of his life, Mephibosheth ate at the king's table with the king's family.

It's a story of extravagant love and undeserved grace. And that's the same grace God extends to you today. It's unearned and undeserved. Believe me, it's not a case of mistaken identity. God handpicked you as the object of his love.

He has a designated place for you at his table; your name is on it. You're welcome to dine with divinity for the rest of your life because you are a member of his family, bona-fide, guaranteed.

Don't worry about the bumps and bruises of your past. Crippled legs are concealed in the father's house, hidden under his table of grace.

And from that time on, Mephibosheth ate regularly at David's table, like one of the king's own sons.
(2 SAMUEL 9:11 NLT)

SIXTY-SIX

The Best Gift of All

A single drop of rain hung suspended from the tip of a pine needle, waiting for the morning breeze to shake it loose. Joshua stood beneath it with his mouth wide open.

"I caught it, Daddy. I caught it."

"Come on, son. Let's go."

The two of them headed down the path to the prophet's house for an unannounced visit. Joshua was all boy, from the top of his curly head to the bottom of his dirty feet. He picked a flower. He splashed a mud puddle. He pocketed a fistful of rocks.

"Drop them, Joshua. You're going to get dirty, and we're almost at Elijah's house."

"Does Lijah like to play?"

"His named is E-lijah. He doesn't play. He's a prophet."

"Why?"

"Because God called him to be a prophet."

"Why?"

"Because God wants his people to hear his message."

"Why?"

"Joshua . . . can you say something besides why?"

"Why?"

They topped the crest of the hill and saw Elijah's house. There he sat on the ground with his head back and his eyes up.

"Shh. Elijah is meditating."

"I'm not meditating, I'm trying to catch a raindrop in my mouth."

"Daddy, Lijah likes to play."

"We apologize for disturbing you, sir. My name is—"

"I know who you are. You are Phinehas the finicky. That's what your wife calls you. Right?"

"Yes, sir, but how did you—"

"You've come today hoping I'll teach the boy how to pray."

"Well, yes. My prayers don't seem to be—"

"Joshua," Elijah said, "give me the eight rocks in your pocket."

Joshua looked up at his dad, embarrassed. Phinehas looked down at his son, ashamed. "All eight. Don't hold back."

"One, two, three," Joshua counted, "four, five, six, seven, eight."

"And the four in the other pocket," Elijah said.

Elijah dragged his finger around the pile of twelve rocks, making a ditch. "This is the way I built the altar on Mount Carmel." He broke a twig into small pieces and let Joshua arrange them on the stones. Then he rolled up a small piece of leather and laid it on top. "Pretend this is a big ole bull, okay? Now give me that jar of water." Elijah poured it over the miniature altar.

"That ain't how you build a fire, Lijah. You need a flint rock like Daddy's got."

"But our God doesn't need flint to build a fire," Elijah said. "He doesn't need clouds to bring rain either. And he doesn't need your worry in order to heal your mommy."

"Why?"

"Because God can do anything, just like he sent fire on my altar at Mount Carmel,"—Elijah slapped the miniature altar with his hand smashing it to the ground—"like that."

"I didn't see no fire," Joshua said.

"Come close and you'll feel the flame." Elijah rubbed his hands together briskly until they were warm. "Feel it?"

"Uh huh."

"Even when you don't see the fire with your eyes, you can still feel it in your heart."

Phinehas gave the prophet a basket of grapes and a bag of cheese, then took his young boy and set out for home.

"Daddy? Is Mama gonna die?"

"I don't know, son. I hope not."

"I wanted to give Mama the flower I picked but I lost it."

"Maybe you can give her the fire in your heart. She needs your love more than anything."

Joshua ran home, climbed in his mom's lap, and gave her a big hug. "Mama, I brought you the best gift of all: the love in my heart."

Love one another.
(JOHN 13:34)

SIXTY-SEVEN

Called by God

The job offer wasn't the kind you negotiate. There was no boss on that side of the desk or applicant on this side of the desk. There was no discussion about salary or working hours. There was no chat about sick days, paid vacations, or personal leave. We didn't talk about company stocks or retirement plans, benefits or bonuses. There was no time for name-dropping, shoulder rubbing, or back-slapping.

Instead, it felt like a done deal, a decision already made. The only wiggle room I had was the space between the back of my mind and the tip of my tongue. How do you say no to a God who says yes? He called, I answered, and that was the end of it. Or I should say the beginning of it.

I thought he should've waited until I was forty. I was only sixteen at the time. Sixteen? Any number with the word teen in it is too young to be a preacher, if you ask me. I was still learning how to pop the pimples on my nose, shave the fuzz off of my lip, and slurp spaghetti off of my chin.

"I have called you unto the labor of ministry." That's what he said. Then he added, "From this day forward you will carry my message to the people whom I chose. I have placed my word in your heart. Do not fear the faces of the people, for I have called you. I will tell you what to say and when to say it. For whom I call, I send, and whom I send, I prepare. And I have prepared you for this hour. Fear none of those things which shall come against you, for you are not alone. I am with you, and if I am with you, who can be against you?"

One gulp and two bats of an eye later, I was a preacher. I had no sermon, no formal training, no mentor, no pulpit, no church, no congregation, and no clue. But I did have a calling. And never underestimate a calling.

When Joshua got his calling, the walls of Jericho fell flat. When

153

Deborah got her calling, the army of the Canaanites fell flat. When David got his calling, Goliath fell flat. When Saul of Tarsus got his calling, he fell flat.

God's call comes with a burden. You don't get one without the other. Don't believe me? Say yes to the call of God, then tell me what happens next. You will feel a weight, like a mantle, drop on your shoulders. You will feel the press of an inward hand on your heart. We call that a burden. Prophets of old tried to describe it (see Ezekiel), while others tried to pass it off to someone else (talk to Moses). One man even tried to outrun the call of God (ask Jonah). But God's call is a divine compulsion that you can't slip or shake.

When God calls you, you begin to see the world like he does. He shares part of his heart with you. Sometimes it makes you laugh. Most of the time it makes you cry. Jeremiah, the weeping prophet, said, "What I see brings grief to my soul" (Lamentations 3:51 NIV).

I didn't understand it as a teenager, but forty years later I'm convinced, the stronger the call, the weaker the quit. Sure, the idea of quitting surfaces from time to time, when the way gets rough and the road gets long, when disappointments mount up and hopes crash down.

Do you want to know what keeps me going when I feel like quitting? What is it that motivates me during the desperate times? It's this single thought: I will let nothing rob me of hearing the One who called me say, "Well *done*, good and faithful servant" (Matthew 25:21).

He who calls you is faithful.
(1 Thessalonians 5:24)

SIXTY-EIGHT

Somebody Prayed

How did I end up in such a horrible place? What a wretched valley. The stench of death is more than I can bear. When the wind blows, I smell the dry fetor of carnage, the decay and corruption of slaughtered millions. Their stench creeps along the valley floor like the fog of war.

At first, it was the smell of death that made me sick. Now it is the waste of vultures and jackals that I loathe. They scattered my bones across this valley without a single thought of mercy. Now all I have to show for it is a memory full of regrets.

I'm dead but not buried. I lie here in the chill of the night without a stitch of clothes. With my right eye, I see ripples of sand in the light of the moon. My left eye looks down, down in the dirt, down to a place worse than this, a place beyond the grave.

My beloved wife and our precious children are here somewhere. Birds of prey fought over their bones. Hyenas carried them off under the cover of night, piece by piece, to some hideous place. I called for them until I lost my voice. O wretched place! How long must I suffer in this pit of pain?

What? A visitor? A sandaled man with olive skin has come to walk among us. His face I cannot see. From here his feet look worn. He's traveled a weary road. He bares the marks of a prophet. How can I tell? It's his staff, his stride, and the somber stillness of his stance. He doesn't run away as others did. He stands. He waits. He cries.

What? A drop of moisture? This is not rain; it is a tear from the man of God. Cry again, sir. The brokenness of your heart gives me hope; the floodgate of your intercession is my escape.

The prophet raises his staff and speaks with authority, "Thus says the Lord GOD to these bones: 'Surely I will cause breath to enter into you, and you shall live'" (Ezekiel 37:5).

Oh yes, dear man, pray and pray again. Call on the God of judgment. Perhaps there is yet a morsel of mercy left for me. Pray, prophet of God. Whatever your name is, it matters not. Just pray.

I hear a clatter now. The earth moves. Pebbles dance. Sand vibrates to the beat of a holy drum. Da-dum. Da-dum. Da-dum. Seraphim fly. Angels chant. The hand of God swirls in the heavens above. A tornado of life rushes past my bones. A vortex of energy blows over my face. Click. Snap. Clack. Pop. My separated bones find their home. I am as I was before. Two hundred and six bones connected piece by piece.

The prophet turns to the eastern sky and prays again. Sinew and muscle cover my bones. Skin cloaks me like a garment.

This time the prophet turns to the west. "Thus says the Lord GOD: 'Come from the four winds, O breath, and breathe on these slain, that they may live'" (Ezekiel 37:9).

WHOOOSH. My lungs fill with air. My eyes pop open. My head snaps forward. An invisible hand lifts me to my feet.

I'm alive. Alive, I say. My wife is by my side. My children stand at my side. The valley breaks forth into laughter. Living bones twirl and dance in celebration.

A shofar blasts. Seraphim hush. Angels salute. The dust in the valley settles, and there we stand, an army prepared for war, rank and file, armed for battle.

"Who was that man?" my daughter asked.

"Ezekiel, the son of Buzi," answered the angel.

"And what was that wind that lifted us up?" my wife asked.

"That was ruach, breath, the Spirit of the living God."

"We're alive again. What just happened?" I asked.

"Somebody prayed," the angel said. "That's what happened, somebody prayed."

So I prophesied as He commanded me,
and breath came into them, and they lived,
and stood upon their feet, an exceedingly great army.
(EZEKIEL 37:10)

SIXTY-NINE

God's Trophy Case

As a young boy growing up, I never had a trophy case. I didn't need one. All I had was two trophies. They sat on the dresser beside my Hot Wheels, G.I. Joe, and football cards.

I was awarded my trophies for playing football and baseball. I was a participant, not a champion; a benchwarmer, not an MVP.

Did you ever receive a trophy? Here's a better question: Did you know that you are a trophy? You are God's trophy.

Here's how Paul described it in his epistle many years ago: "God can point to us in all future ages as examples of the incredible wealth of his grace and kindness" (Ephesians 2:7 NLT).

The fact that God points to us as examples of his grace tells me he has a trophy case. It's not a single shelf behind glass where he displays the busts of his favorite saints. No, I'm talking about a magnificent room, a hall of fame, a corridor of champions. It's lined with proof after proof of saints who reflect his amazing grace. Take a walk with me, and you'll see for yourself.

"Ah, there's Abraham," you say. He straddles a rock altar with a knife in his hand. Isaac lays beneath him. An angel stands beside him. It's his moment on Mount Moriah. At times, God points to this trophy of Abraham to prove that true love and obedience supersedes personal passion.

"And there's Moses at the Red Sea." His staff is outstretched, his hair windblown, and his eyes fixated. Walls of water stand at attention on both sides as a nation of slaves march toward a land of freedom. It's a moment in time, a display of divinity, and another proof of God's grace and goodness.

We take a few more steps down the corridor of champions and see Deborah under a palm tree, Jael with a mallet and a tent peg, David with a sling, and Elijah with his mantle.

Since we don't have time to ponder each and every trophy, I

hurry you along, wanting you to see what's in the last room. We rush past trophies of Peter and Andrew, Paul and Silas, and John on the Island of Patmos.

In the next room, without slowing down, we blur right past Polycarp, Augustine, Luther, Calvin, and Wesley. But you slow down when you see Fanny Crosby. She's hunched over a writing desk, penning the words of a song: "Blessed assurance, Jesus is mine! Oh, what a foretaste of glory divine!"

Across the hall, Billy Graham preaches at a crusade in New York, and Reinhard Bonnke prays for souls in Kenya.

"Come quickly," I say. "This is what I want you to see."

We step into the last room. You gasp. It's a trophy of you. There you are in God's trophy case, right where you belong. He proudly displays your life as proof of his grace.

You stand there in shock, hand over mouth. "I didn't know I was one of God's trophies."

Read the label. It has the date you were born again. It proves God is merciful to sinners. Your name inscribed on the bottom matches your name in the Book of Life.

He points to you when he defends his grace to people who think he is unjust. Before they look to Jesus on the cross, they see you at school, at work, and at home. Your life points them to Jesus.

How can they see God's grace? By looking at you, because you are God's trophy on display for others to see that he is gracious.

You're no benchwarmer. You are God's MVP.

Let your light shine before others, that they may see your good deeds and glorify your Father in heaven.
(MATTHEW 5:16 NIV)

SEVENTY

The Perfect Christmas

Shame on me for wanting a perfect Christmas. It's a tiny bit selfish and an itsy bit snide, but it's what I want: the perfect gift, wrapped in perfect paper, under the perfect tree, topped with a perfect star. And while I'm at it, I'll request perfect mistletoe overhead and a perfect wife in my arms.

I'll be happy as long as Nat King Cole sings about chestnuts roasting on an open fire, but don't mess up my Christmas by telling me Grandma got run over by a reindeer. I want children snug in their beds with sugar plums dancing in their heads. Don't you? Of course you do. We want jingle bells and one-horse open sleighs. Give us fruitcake, for goodness sake. That's the stuff Christmases are made of, right?

Wrong. Nothing's perfect, including Christmas. Trees that should stand tall lean against the wall. Blinking lights quit blinking, unbreakable toys break, and *batteries not included* means "I forgot to buy the batteries."

Christmas is full of surprises and not always the good kind. Sometimes Christmas includes broken promises and broken hearts, separation and divorce, or funeral homes and cemeteries.

"But I don't want that kind of Christmas," you say. "I want the perfect kind."

"Like the one in the Bible?"

"Yes, like the first Christmas, the original one."

"Oh yeah. Take another look. It wasn't so perfect."

"Then Herod, when he saw that he was deceived by the wise men, was exceedingly angry; and he sent forth and put to death all the male children who were in Bethlehem" (Matthew 2:16).

I thought Christmas was supposed to be about a Messiah in a manger, not murder and mayhem. How did a slaughter of children get in this story? Christmas should be about Jack Frost, not Jack the Ripper. Shepherds and wise men? Yes. Mercenaries and hatchet men? No. We don't like this part of the Christmas story, but it's in the Bible and we can't deny it.

The same Christmas that includes the birth of baby Jesus includes the death of other babies. While the mother from Nazareth cried with joy, mothers throughout Bethlehem wept with grief. Mary wrapped her baby in swaddling clothes; they wrapped their babies in burial clothes.

"Well, I didn't see that one coming."

"Me neither, but Jeremiah did."

"A voice was heard in Ramah, Lamentation *and* bitter weeping, Rachel weeping for her children" (Jeremiah 31:15).

We don't have to be prophets in order to understand that Christmas isn't supposed to be perfect, and this year's Christmas is tainted more than most. Some of our friends and family died in the last twelve months. Others are quarantined. Some are in hospitals. Others are overseas. Some are out of work. Others can't get off of work. Some grocery stores are closed or limited in stock, so favorite recipes won't be made this year. We've become a society of mask wearers six feet away from hugs and kisses. We are surrounded with political tension, global unrest, economic uncertainty, and viral pandemics. Yet, in some ways, this imperfect Christmas resembles the first Christmas more than all of the Christmases of the past.

Think about it. Pregnant Mary rode a bony-back donkey up and down ninety miles of turns and twists in the heat of day and the cold of night. Eventually, she laid down on a hay-strewn floor in a roughhewn cave designed to shelter animals. Her labor and delivery room was not sanitized. Her doctor was not credentialed. Her nurse was not trained. Anesthesia was not available. She had no baby bottles, no heated lamps, no pacifiers, and no Pampers. She gave birth to a brand-new baby in the old-fashioned way. She pushed, pulled, sweated, and screamed. The floor was dirty. The walls were dank. The night was dark. That's when the impossible became possible, and on that imperfect Christmas, the perfect One was born.

When her child is born, her anguish gives way to joy because she has brought a new baby into the world.
(John 16:21 NLT)

SEVENTY-ONE

Lovesick

The front door closes behind me, and I fight back the tears, just like the last hundred times. Another work week is another week away from home. So I turn up the radio and roll down the window. I grab a coffee on my way out of town. It's supposed to make me feel better, but beneath all the tricks and charades, my lovesick heart breaks, in secret, in silence. No one knows. No one but me and the teary guy in the mirror.

I spend the night in a dingy motel room with worn carpet and thin towels. Drab pictures hang on pale walls. The TV is bolted to the dresser. Clothes racks are cuffed to the closet rod. What is this, a prison?

A stranger will deliver a pizza for ten bucks, but it's not the face of a stranger I want to see. It's the face of a friend I need the most: the friend whose face was behind the veil when I said I do, the face I see when I close my eyes. But she's miles away, and I'm stuck in this place without her.

I sit in a stiff chair beside a cracked window and peer through a hazy fog. Gray clouds cover dreary skies. Spring rains pound the parking lot. Traffic lights blink blurry colors.

I see a couple walking in the rain, one man and one woman under an umbrella. Does he know how lucky he is to have her by his side? I watch from an empty room, with a lonely heart.

Then my phone rings. It's her. My world brightens. Her voice is calm; her hello is sweet. I realize I'm not alone. We're separated physically, yes, but we're still together. Miles apart but sharing the same stories, winking at the same moon, laughing at the same jokes.

When the week is over, I can't wait to get home. The closer I get, the faster I drive. I pull into the driveway and trot up the steps. I open the door and see her on the couch. I can breathe again. I can walk on air now. All my problems vanish in her arms. For the next forty-eight hours, I'm a kid in a candy store.

Crazy? Probably. Over the top? Maybe, but don't knock it until you've tried it. Whoever said there's no such thing as love has never been in love. And if you have been in love, you've experienced a little bit of heaven on earth, just like me. And Jacob.

Jacob who? The guy in the Bible who fell in love with Rachel. It was love at first sight. He flipped. She flipped. And together they just flopped, head over heels in love. He was dashing and daring. She was drop-dead gorgeous.

Jacob's first question was, "Will you marry me?" His second question was, "What is your name?" He was lovesick to the core.

Per their custom, Jacob had to work seven years for the right to marry Rachel. Rake hay. Feed cows. Mend fences. Now repeat it again every day for two thousand days. Every drop of sweat, every aching back, every weary bone, and every sleepless night was worth it. That's how true love thinks.

They tricked Jacob on the wedding day and hitched him up with Rachel's sister, Leah. That's like falling in love with Cinderella but marrying Drizella. How do you say yucky in Hebrew?

Jacob had to work seven more years to marry Rachel. Most guys would rather scrape their eyes out with a rusty fork. But not Jacob.

"So Jacob worked seven years to pay for Rachel. But his love for her was so strong that it seemed to him but a few days" (Genesis 29:20 NLT). That's love on another level.

But there's a higher level of love yet, a love greater than Jacob's love for Rachal. There is a love so grand, so good, and so glorious that it forsook a beautiful heaven to embrace a blemished earth—a love that exchanged regal robes and royal diadems for thorny crowns and Roman nails; a love that looks beyond our faults and failures, beyond our guile and guilt; a love for Drizella as much as Cinderella.

Where is this love? Who is this lover? His name is Jesus, and he loves you with a perfect love, even when you're not so perfect.

Greater love has no one than this,
than to lay down one's life for his friends.
(JOHN 15:13)

SEVENTY-TWO

A Different Passover

Mary folded enough clothes for the whole family, calling each child's name as she stuffed garments in the basket. "Here's one for Jesus, one for James, Joseph, Judas, Simon—" Her train of thought was interrupted by two of her boys picking on their sister. "Stop!" Mary snapped her finger. "We're leaving in a few minutes. We don't have time to play. Where's your father?" Ten-year-old James shrugged a shoulder.

Joseph was outside tying luggage in a bundle. Jesus stood beside him, steadying the donkey.

"Son, Passover will be different for you this year," Joseph said, as if Jesus didn't already know. "You're twelve now. You're becoming a man, so you have to do what grown men do. Understand?"

"Yes, sir. I'm supposed to kill the lamb this year. I know." Jesus whispered as he gently rubbed the donkey's ears.

"Are you nervous about it?" Joseph asked.

Jesus shook his head no, then blinked fast to keep tears from spilling, "It's not my will, but if it's your will, I'll do it." Joseph pulled the rope, made a knot, and wondered if Jesus was up to it.

Soon they were on the road (Joseph, Mary, and a cartload of kids). Streams of families flowed out of every town and village of Galilee, headed south for the annual feast. The closer they got to Jerusalem, the louder they sang the songs of David, except for Jesus. He walked quietly by himself, gazing off into the distance with something heavy on his mind.

Pilgrims and travelers poured into Jerusalem from every quarter. Makeshift markets lined the roads, street vendors peddled their wares, boys and girls jumped rope in the grass, moms and dads set up tents, and excited worshippers filed into the temple to hear the Levite choir.

The next morning when Joseph went to wake up Jesus, he found him awake sitting outside the tent and writing something on the ground with his finger. "Are you alright, son? Are you ready for the sacrifice today?"

"I am. I am," he said twice.

The two of them walked to the Temple to purchase a lamb. Joseph gave the redemption money to Jesus, then nodded toward the priest. Jesus paid the price without reservation, like he knew what he was doing. "Bless you, young man," the priest said. "Now pick any lamb you want; there's not a spot or a blemish among them." Jesus waded knee-deep into a flock of lambs. His legs brushed against their warm bodies. He knew they'd all be dead before the sun went down.

"This one," Jesus said.

"Are you sure?" Joseph asked.

"Yes." Jesus held the lamb in his arms. "Look how peaceful he is. He knows he was born to die." At the altar, Jesus rubbed his fingers through its wool one last time, whispered a prayer, and made the fatal incision.

The priest caught the blood in a basin, sprinkled the altar, and hung the lamb on a post with its limbs spread apart. Joseph carried one end and Jesus carried the other. When the weight of the sacrifice fell on his shoulder, Jesus closed his eyes and grimaced.

Later that evening, the family reunited for the Passover meal. Joseph turned around just in time to see Jesus standing in front of his siblings. His arms were stretched out wide on each side, and his chin dropped dead on his chest. "Jesus, what kind of game are you playing?"

Jesus answered, "I'm not playing games. I'm showing them what a slain lamb looks like."

You were not redeemed with corruptible things . . . but with
the precious blood of Christ, as of a lamb without blemish.
(1 PETER 1:18-19)

SEVENTY-THREE

Ready to Go

His face bore the marks of ninety winters, and his hair clung to his head like old snow on a rugged mountain. His teeth were gone, like most of his memory, but his smile lingered with his old age. Although I didn't know what he was laughing about, I laughed with him. The doctor said he didn't have long to live.

His wife and daughter stepped out of the room for a quick lunch. I promised to stay with him until they returned. It was a forty-minute experience I'll never forget. He slept in the bed. I sat in the chair. Before I could read a few pages of my book, he woke up mumbling. I patted him on the back of the hand and assured him he wasn't alone.

"I know," he chuckled. "I'm not. I know. He's there, right there." He closed his eyes and started snoring again. I untangled the IV cord and covered his feet with a blanket.

The book I'd been reading told about the accounts of people who had died briefly and came back to life. Some encountered angels, others saw heaven or their loved ones who had gone on before. Just as I reached to pick up my book from the windowsill, the old man gasped. I thought he was dying on the spot.

"No, don't die on me. Your wife's not here."

He leaned forward and sat up in bed with strength I didn't know he had. His eyes widened, his mouth fell open with a toothless grin, and his arms reached out in front of him. His dinner tray, with a cup of water, was on a cart under the TV.

"Are you thirsty?" I took a step toward his tray.

"Here he comes. Do you see him?"

The old man looked beyond me, beyond the foot of the bed, and beyond the reality of that room. His eyes were focused on something unseen, someone invisible.

"Who is it?"

"He's beautiful. Dressed in light, glorious light. Here he comes. I'm ready. I'm ready to go." Those were his last words on earth. His next words were in another place, a place out of this world. He died a few hours later with his wife by his side.

I shared his final words at the funeral a few days later. "Thurston was a man of faith. His last words were, 'I'm ready to go.'"

His wife told me that he gave his heart to the Lord back in 1927. He wouldn't wait for Sunday, so they walked to the preacher's house on Saturday. In the pastor's living room, he surrendered his life to Jesus Christ. Before the sun went down, the preacher baptized him in the swimming hole.

That was the day he got ready to go. And he stayed ready until it was his time to go.

If you're not ready to go, what are you waiting for? Jesus is ready. He's just waiting on you.

To everything there is a season, . . .
a time to be born, and a time to die.
(ECCLESIASTES 3:1-2)

SEVENTY-FOUR

Servant of All

Peter pushed through the front door as boisterous as ever. "I'm home," he yelled. Before his wife could dry her dishpan hands, he shouted again, "What's for dinner?"

She blew her sweaty bangs off to one side and smiled through her exhaustion. "Dinner? I didn't know you were coming home today." She stood on her tiptoes and wrapped her damp arms around his sun-dried neck. Hidden beneath his burly mustache and deep-set eyes was the tender man she fell in love with years ago. She closed her eyes and kissed him. "Welcome home, stranger."

Peter nudged his nose against her ear and whispered, "The whole gang's with me. Thirteen of us."

She dropped to her heels with a thud. "How am I supposed to feed thirteen men, plus me, mom, and the kids? Food is scarce."

Peter kicked his sandals off in the corner and shrugged. "You'll manage. You always do." He stuck his head outside and gave a nod. A dozen rowdy men paraded through her kitchen like a boatload of drifters at the first sight of land. Jesus, the last one in, was kind enough to close the door.

Peter's five-year-old boy hid behind his mother, afraid of the ruffians. "Don't be scared, sweetie," his mother said. "They're nice men." But it was too late; the little boy was already spooked. Uncle Andrew's face bore a permanent scar, Philip's hair looked like dead men's fingers, Judas's eyes danced with demons, and Thomas's lumbering stride reminded him of Goliath. Only Jesus got a smile out of him. A sorghum drop and a playful wink did the trick.

Peter's wife and mother-in-law pulled enough scraps together to mimic a meal, while the men did what men do best: fight over the Lazy Boy and the remote control (well, sort of). Peter grabbed the best chair (it was his house, you know). Four guys squeezed onto the couch, six sat on throw pillows, and the last two made a move for the child-size rocker. James got there first, so Jesus politely sat on the floor, servant style.

While pots and pans rattled in the kitchen, disciples squabbled in the living room, bragging about who caught the most fish, who performed the most miracles, and who deserved to sit beside Jesus in the new kingdom. After points were calculated, Peter polished his fingernails on his shirt. "I'm the only among us who walked on water." John cringed. James croaked. The other disciples caved.

"Does Peter always have to be first?" his wife's mom whispered.

The wife rolled her eyes as she rolled the biscuits. "First and right. It's a combination that requires a lot of patience."

Jesus cleared his throat to get their attention. He motioned for Peter's son, who ran to his side and sat by him on the floor. "Whoever wants to be first must take last place and be the servant of everyone else" (Mark 9:35 NLT). Jesus wrapped his arm around the boy and pulled him close. "Anyone who welcomes a little child like this on my behalf welcomes me, and anyone who welcomes me welcomes not only me but also my Father who sent me" (Mark 9:37 NLT).

"No one offered to wash feet when we arrived. No one volunteered for kitchen duty? None of you gave up your seat for your brother?" Peter squirmed. James blushed. "In my kingdom the first are last, and the last are first. Who is the greatest? The one who is servant of all. Erase your scorecard. Count like your heavenly Father does, from the bottom up, not from the top down. Serving Others is the name of the game. So, who is the winner now?" (Crickets.)

To break the silence, Peter's wife announced, "Dinner is served." Peter bolted from his chair to get to the front of the line. John raised an eyebrow. James pretended to cough. The little boy looked up at Jesus and asked, "Was Daddy listening at all?"

"Of course he was. Your daddy is a good man."

Peter returned to the living room with an armload of dinner plates. "Keep your seats, brothers, I'll bring it to you. And Jesus, please take my chair; you're the guest of honor."

"Yay," the little boy shouted. He hugged his daddy around the waist. "You can have my sorghum drop."

Everyone clapped and the whole house filled with laughter.

So the last will be first, and the first last.
(MATTHEW 20:16)

168

SEVENTY-FIVE

Legalism or Love

I once met a preacher who was as mean as the devil. His back was straight, his eyes were straight, his finger was straight, and his preaching was straight. If you didn't live it just like he preached it, you were going to Hell.

His flavor of Christianity was bitter from the first bite. He never smiled, and if you did, shame on you. Any hair that touched your ear or your collar would send you to Hell. His hair was crew cut, and he expected mine to be the same. I was nineteen years old and had to spend a week with this guy. I've been bald ever since.

In the early days of my ministry, every road I took led me to a place I'd never been. Every opportunity to preach introduced me to people I'd never met. They'd look at me like, "Where'd this guy come from?" And I'd look at them like, "The sooner I get out of here the better." How I survived a run through that gauntlet, I'll never know. It must have been the prayers of the saints and the grace of God.

After my first sermon in that guy's church, he told the people, "Come on back tomorrow night. It's bound to get better." He didn't know I'd already preached my best sermon.

I wondered why the pastor and his wife were sad all of the time. They never laughed, never smiled, and never looked happy about anything. Was it because they had to cook on an old wood stove or because they never had new clothes to wear? I don't know, but by the end of the week, I'd learned not to laugh or smile either.

The preacher wanted me to preach hell, fire, and brimstone. It pleased him when I did and disappointed him when I didn't. When the revival meeting finally ended, he patted me on the back and said, "You come back next year, and we'll make a good preacher out of you yet."

I headed to my next meeting with a quandary of questions. Had

I been wrong all this time? Did I need to learn how to "shake the bushes" and "put the fear of God in people" like he told me to?

"Stand tall, raise your voice, and look them straight in the eye. Jerk a knot in them if you have to." That was his advice, but it ran contrary to what I'd been doing, and I was confused.

My next revival meeting was in a totally different place. Everybody smiled. I thought, "What's wrong with these people? Don't they know you shouldn't do that?"

I had my work cut out for me that week. I'd planned to shake the bushes and run the devil out of that place before it was over. However, my plan got sidetracked by the pastor's wife.

She was the nicest lady I'd ever met. Her voice was motherly, her eyes were compassionate, her touch was gentle, her prayer was heavenly, and her flavor of Christianity was sweeter than a honeycomb.

I watched her weep with struggling souls at the altar. I listened to her teach about the love of Jesus in Sunday school class. I heard her sing praises to the Lord while cooking in the kitchen. I followed along as she read her Bible at the breakfast table each morning.

By the end of the week, that motherly saint had persuaded me that the best way to win people to Jesus was to love them in, not scare them in.

Ever since then, I quit shaking bushes. Instead, I started preaching Christ crucified, buried, and resurrected. It took me a while to figure it out, but I've learned, a tear in the eye is better than a fist in the air, and a helping hand is better than a kick in the britches.

The one who does not love does not
know God, because God is love.
(1 JOHN 4:8 NASB)

SEVENTY-SIX

Touching Jesus

She fluffed her makeshift pillow and tried to go back to sleep, but the morning dew was too thick. She was wet from head to toe. The ground was hard. The night was cold. She'd survived a thousand nights like this; surely she could outlast one more.

She was one of hundreds sleeping under the black sky on that never-ending night. They all waited for the same thing: the rising of the sun and the return of the Rabbi. Jesus and his disciples had sneaked away the night before, leaving the crowd in Capernaum to fend for themselves. Like a flock of scattered sheep, they shuffled in the grass along the northern slope of Lake Gennesaret, waiting for him to come back. The blind, the deaf, the frail, and the forgotten—each hoped to gain audience with the One who could make a difference, the One whose touch heals every hurt.

Her visit to Capernaum was a final effort to find a cure. No doctor could help. No medicine could cure. Salves, ointments, potions, and concoctions—she'd tried them all, from sitting over pots of boiling leaves to bathing in mud from the Dead Sea. Nothing worked. She was out of money and out of time.

She traveled to Capernaum because she'd heard a certain man was there: a holy man, a healer. Her final hope rested in this Rabbi. If he couldn't help her, nobody could. By the time she arrived, he'd already left. She spent the longest night of her life roiling in pain without so much as a single star to wish away her worries.

Long at last, the morning sun broke over Gadara's mount and unmasked a fisherman's boat slipping through the shallows. Before Jesus could step out of the boat and clear the dock, the clamoring crowd surrounded him with demands for healing.

Jairus, ruler of the synagogue, had the upper hand. He was at the front of the line. Others had to wait their turn, including the desperate woman at the back of the line. She wrapped her thin coat around her frail body and pressed into the crowd. "Perhaps if I could get close enough to see his face . . . if he would simply look my way and sense my pain . . . ," she thought.

Disappointment struck again. Jesus turned in the opposite direction. Jairus had the Rabbi's attention and was leading him back into town. She tried getting closer, but the people were in her way. She wriggled and wrestled, pushed and pressed. "Excuse me, please. Pardon me." Her words were polite, but her actions were provocative. She fought through the fray like a salmon swimming upstream.

The narrow streets of Capernaum thinned out the crowd. Not wanting to make a scene, she decided to "steal" her healing. "She thought to herself, 'If I can just touch his robe, I will be healed'" (Mark 5:28 NLT). His tallit tassels trailed behind him, swinging freely with every step. If she timed it just right, she could brush her hand against the fringe. No one would know the difference. She bent low, as if to pick up something from the ground, and stretched her hand forward. One finger touched one thread, and BAM! A bolt of lightning surged through her body and took her breath away. She froze in place as the crowd stepped around her.

"Who touched my robe?" Jesus said as he spun on his heels. Shocked, the whole crowd denied it. They understood protocol: No one is to touch a Rabbi in public. His eyes widened. His voice sharpened. "Somebody touched me!" As everyone took a step back, distancing themselves from the accusation, the woman spoke up. On her knees with her face in her hands, she admitted, "It was me." She prepared for her reprimand and dismissal. She'd been kicked out of town before. This wouldn't be the first time.

Jesus stooped down to her level and picked a piece of grass out of her hair. He looked into her fearful eyes and said, "'You are now well because of your faith. . . . You are healed, and you will no longer be in pain' (Mark 5:34 CEV). Your plague is mine, my peace is yours. Welcome home."

As the crowd continued down the road, she sat in the dust, amazed at what just happened. "I thought I didn't have a friend in the world but found out I have family in Jesus."

Go in peace. Your suffering is over.
(Mark 5:34 NLT)

SEVENTY-SEVEN

Father's Day

The value of a father is rarely appreciated until he's gone. Uncles are great. Cousins are nice. Pastors are helpful. But only Dad can be Dad.

If yours is like mine, he taught you lots of stuff: how to walk, how to ride a bike, how to throw a baseball, and how not to cry over spilled milk or scraped knees. Dad also taught me that money doesn't grow on trees, hard work never killed anyone, and it'll be alright before you get married (ever hear that one?). Dad taught me how to fish and hunt, how to change a tire and check the oil, how to shave and tie a necktie.

The first dad God created was Adam. He made him out of dirt and told him to tend a garden. But Adam had no toolshed. He didn't own boots or bibbed overalls. He had no string or stakes, no picks or pails, no shovels or rakes. Ace Hardware hadn't been invented and Craftsman didn't exist. How was Adam supposed to tend a garden? Simple. God gave him all the stuff it takes to be a dad, so tending a garden was a piece of cake. Dads come prewired with eyebrows to catch sweat, fingernails to get dirty, knees to bend down, backbone to stand up, and a song to whistle while they work.

Adam didn't own screwdrivers and wrenches or wheel barrels and ladders. But he did own grit, and he was the first guy to get it in his teeth. Fathering and gardening both require elbow grease, so God gave Adam two elbows. Adam had to find the grease himself. And he did, in the same place I found mine—on the inside. It comes with fatherhood.

Dads have to fix lots of things: broken toys, broken windows, and broken hearts. That's why God gave them strong hands; they're designed to hold things together. God also gave them broad shoulders. They're made for sons to ride on and daughters to lean on.

Speaking of kids, when Eve found out she was pregnant, she said, "We're going to need a nursery."

Adam said, "Sure, right after I build a shelter for my John Deere."

"What's a John Deere?"

"A tractor and the name of our first son."

She *raised Cane*, and that was the end of that conversation.

Father's Day is a designated holiday to honor dads. It was placed on the calendar for a reason. It's a single day in June when every son or daughter in the world pause long enough to show appreciation to their father. Dads don't need cards or flowers like moms do. They don't need party balloons or elaborate dinners. Most dads can function in their role without a lot of fussing and fuming, as long as they hear these two words every once in a while: "Thanks, Dad." Those two words sound like, "Gentlemen, start your engines." There's no task too big, no challenge too great. When a father hears, "Thanks Dad," he inhales courage and exhales pride. He's ready to ride the wind and lasso the moon.

So whether it is June or July, rain or shine, day or night, if you want your dad to feel like the greatest man on earth, here's what you do: Climb up on his lap, wrap your arms around his neck, put your lips close to his ear, and whisper those two magic words, "Thanks Dad." (Then you can ask him to do anything in the whole wide world, and he'll do it. Guaranteed.)

As a father has compassion on his children,
so the LORD has compassion on those who fear him.
(PSALM 103:13 NIV)

SEVENTY-EIGHT

The Triumphal Entry

On the first day of the festival, crowds poured into Jerusalem from every quarter. The population swelled by the hour. Local Judeans arrived first, followed by Galileans, and then by other worshippers scattered throughout the Diaspora. Every Jewish holiday reminded Israel that her promised Messiah would come, but no event on the calendar sparked hopes more than Passover.

This year, excitement was at an all-time high. A prophet from Nazareth named Jesus had recently raised a man from the dead. Only the Messiah could do such a thing. Would he make his grand entrance into Jerusalem during the feast and claim ownership to the throne? As a safeguard against such possibilities, Rome increased its military presence. Religious uprisings would not be tolerated.

With the pomp of a Roman governor, Pontius Pilate strode into the city through its western gate. Armed soldiers, mounted on gallant horses, led the grand procession. Pilate opened the curtains on his canopied carriage so spectators could see his arrival. Israel must not forget its rightful place under his iron fist and beneath his idol gods. But this Passover week there was a challenger in the wings.

About the same time Pilate rolled into Jerusalem from the west, another procession began to form on the east. A Galilean known as a miracle worker, a demon chaser, and a water walker was on his way to town. He rode on a donkey along the old caravan route from Bethphage. Reminiscent of King Solomon, son of David, Jesus's triumphal entry into Jerusalem reminded Israel of her glory days.

On the western side of the city, horses pranced, but on the eastern side a donkey plodded. On the west red carpet lined the rode, but on the east palm branches covered the path. On the west soldiers guarded their governor, but on the east children worshipped their king. On the west a Roman announced his authority, but on the east a Jew declared his deity. On the west Pilate eyed the capitol, but on the east Jesus had his sights set on the cross.

What a sight. An unrivaled king on an untamed donkey, parading over strewn palm branches and surrounded by a wave of worship. It was a scene, and a sign, Israel had waited to see for centuries. It had been prophesied over five hundred years before. "Shout, O daughter of Jerusalem! Behold, your King is coming to you . . . riding on a donkey" (Zechariah 9:9).

Galilean pilgrims traveled with Jesus down the dusty road through the Kidron Valley, singing, "I was glad when they said unto me, let us go into the house of the LORD" (Psalm 122:1 KJV). Judean locals waited for his arrival near the eastern gate, singing a different song. "Blessed *is* he who comes in the name of the LORD!" (Psalm 118:26). When the two crowds merged into one, Hosannas reached the highest heavens. Rings of children danced and sang. Fathers and mothers shouted for joy. Jerusalem erupted into praise. "Lift up your heads, O you gates! And be lifted up, you everlasting doors! And the King of glory shall come in" (Psalm 24:7).

Amidst all the messianic worship, some misguided Pharisees balked and chided. "Teacher, rebuke your followers for saying things like that!" (Luke 19:39 NLT).

Jesus didn't budge an inch. "If they kept quiet, the stones along the road would burst into cheers!" (Luke 19:40 NLT).

For three-and-a-half years, Jesus had quieted the people who would make him known because his time had not yet come. But Palm Sunday was the turning point. His time was now. He changed his public policy. Since then, believers all around the world are encouraged to make his praise glorious, shout it from the rooftops, and proclaim it in the city streets.

> *Praise him, praise him! Jesus, our blessed redeemer!*
> *Sing, O earth, his wonderful love proclaim!*
> *Hail him, hail him! Highest archangels in glory!*
> *Strength and honor give to his holy name!*
> (FANNY CROSBY)[1]

Blessed is He who comes in the name of the LORD!
(JOHN 12:13)

SEVENTY-NINE

Walk and Not Faint

Nervous jitters raced through my mind like a lit fuse. It was only a matter of time before they exploded, knocked me off my feet, and left me on the floor like a bag of bones: unconscious, uncivilized, and unsightly.

I don't do well with doctors, needles, blood, or pain. I've locked those childhood monsters away in a dark closet, and cursed be the one who lets them out. I've fainted in dentists' chairs and doctors' offices, at blood drives and in vaccine lines. Do you want to see me squirm? Point a sharp needle toward my arm or any other place that recoils at the thought of hypodermic intrusion, and you'll find me in the floor quicker than a hiccup. That's why I held on to the bed rails in the hospital one unforgettable morning many years ago.

My pastor friend and I were doing what ministers are expected to do: visiting the sick. I didn't ask any questions when he said, "Let's visit one of my members on the way to lunch." How was I supposed to know the guy was in traction, in ICU, with his leg chained to the ceiling, torture-style? A warning would've been good. A detour for an oxygen mask would've been better.

The patient had been in a car accident and was wrapped up like a mummy with only his nose and toes exposed. A paper bag full of smelling salts could not have prevented what happened next.

My knees swung in directions never intended. My stomach danced in my throat to the tune of "Can't Stop Me Now." And my head played hide-and-seek with my feet. When I woke up, with my head under the bed, I had created a new game in the hospital: ICU But You Can't See Me. The pastor stopped praying for the other guy and started praying for me. Now I know why wheelchairs are provided in medical centers—to roll wimps outside for fresh air.

Fast forward a few years to the time my wife said, "I want you to go with me in the labor and delivery room."

I gnarled my face, squinted my eyes, cocked my head, and said,

"You want me to do whaaaat? Of all people, you know I can't do that."

"Pray about it," she said.

"Sure, I'll pray about it," I said, knowing full well God understood my problem.

"Lord, you know I don't do hospitals and I'm not going in that labor room. Please tell my wife so she won't be mad."

"My son, I am with you, even in the labor room."

"No, Lord. I'll end up in the floor. I don't want my child to know I fainted at the first sight of him."

"I have a word for you. Get your Bible," the Lord said.

I found my Bible. It fell open to Isaiah 40, one of my favorite chapters. I sat down, caught my breath, and started reading. "Even the youths shall faint" (Isaiah 40:30).

"See, Lord. It's right there. I'm young and I faint. I told you."

"Keep reading," the Lord said.

"And the young men shall utterly fall" (Isaiah 40:30). "There it is again, Lord. I told you I'd fall in the floor."

"Keep reading."

"But those who wait on the LORD shall renew *their* strength; they shall mount up with wings like eagles, they shall run and not be weary, they shall walk and not faint" (Isaiah 40:31).

There it is," he said.

"What? Where? I don't get it."

"The last phrase. It's right in front of you. Just believe it."

I read it again. "They shall walk and not faint."

That was over thirty years ago, and I'm still standing on that promise. Since then, I've learned how to enter hospitals and exit on my own two feet. I've learned how to face doctors' reports and shrug a shoulder. I've learned how to stand beside coffins and sing "Amazing Grace." And I've learned how to walk into the ICU by keeping my eyes on H-I-M.

What's the secret? It's that last phrase, right in front of you. "Walk and not faint."

They shall run and not be weary,
they shall walk and not faint.
(ISAIAH 40:31)

EIGHTY

Silent No More

The fire in Caiaphas's courtyard fizzled and popped as burning branches crumbled into coals. Servants of the High Priest huddled close to the flames and rubbed the chill out of their bones. Jesus stood farther back in chains; his feet fettered, and his hands tied. From the moment they had arrested him in Gethsemane, he hadn't said a word. Half naked and barefooted, he shivered in the predawn shadows.

The amber glow on his face revealed a bloody nose and a bruised cheek. His bloodshot eyes transfixed on something in the distance: a man hiding near the courtyard gate, a fellow Galilean, a personal friend, a disciple named Peter. At that instant, a rooster crowed. Their eyes met across the expanse of the torchlit compound. Peter froze, then fled quicker than a broken promise. All Jesus could do was weep for his friend, a friend who felt like life wasn't worth living.

"Let's go," a Sanhedrin member shouted. A small contingent of religious leaders stepped out of the warm palace into the chilly air. The convoy was headed to Pilate's praetorium. They carried formal accusations in hand, hoping for a quick execution. The man who claimed to be the Messiah must die today. Passover began at sundown, and there was no time to waste.

Jesus's fettered feet slowed them down, but they refused to wait. They dragged him through the narrow streets of Jerusalem, sneaking through the residential district before the sun came up. The rogue Rabbi had been a thorn in their side long enough. Pilate's verdict would shut him up for good.

The Sanhedrin envoys stopped at the praetorium's perimeter. (Holy sandals can't step on unholy soil.) When Pilate met them at the property line, he saw right through their charade. The petition for execution was clearly biased, hardly worth wasting a Roman minute. But at the behest of Caiaphas, he entertained their charges.

"When the leading priests and the elders made their accusations against him, Jesus remained silent" (Matthew 27:12 NLT). Silent? Really? Why didn't he say something, anything?

Don't mistake his silence for weakness. He wasn't intimidated or afraid. He wasn't dumbfounded or delirious. He wasn't flabbergasted or tongue-tied. Jesus could have defended himself with no problem. He had every legal right to argue his case.

Perhaps Moses said, "If he only had my staff." Gideon said, "If he only had my torch." David said, "If he only had my sling." Elijah said, "If he only had my mantle." But God said, "He already has my plan. That's all he needs."

At any given moment, if he wanted to, Jesus could've snapped his fingers and stopped the whole charade. He could've pushed the panic button, and heaven would've bailed him out. He could've turned the flimsy reed into a scepter of power. He could've ditched the scarlet robe and slipped into Shekinah. He could've tossed aside the crown of thorns and put on a royal diadem. With a simple whisper, a myriad of angels would've swooped down to rescue him. But he chose to remain silent.

Fear didn't silence his voice before Caiaphas. Dignity did. Chains didn't restrain him from running after Peter. Wisdom did. Barabbas didn't force him to go to Skull Hill. Destiny did. Fetters didn't hold him to the whipping post. Compassion did. The cross didn't buckle his knees. Sin did. The nails didn't hold him on the tree. Love did. The Roman seal didn't keep him in the tomb. Prophecy did. The disciples didn't free him from the grave. God did.

When it was all over—Jesus stood triumphant. He endured it all. He conquered it all. And then, he was silent no more.

I am he who lives, and was dead,
and behold, I am alive forevermore.
(REVELATION 1:18)

EIGHTY-ONE

Goose Talk

It's a marvel of nature.

Twice every year the skies along the eastern seaboard come alive with Canadian geese. Like college students on winter break, they flock by the millions to warm waters in the south. Then, in the spring, they reverse course and head back home to the north. Long strands of black-and-white birds stretch out for miles in the open air, playing the grandest game of follow-the-leader you'll ever see.

At first glance it looks chaotic, but keep watching; you'll see teamwork at its finest. These geese are no dodo birds. They are brilliant strategist. They line up in a V formation and flap their wings with the synchrony of a marching band.

Each goose flies at the wingtip of its flight partner, taking advantage of the upwash of air produced by the goose up front. This strategy reduces wind resistance and allows the flock to fly much farther together than they could fly alone.

It's not only a sight to see, it's a commotion to hear. To the untrained ear, the quacking and honking sounds like pandemonium, but once you learn goose talk, it sounds like, "Hey, Mom, you're doing great. We'll be there in no time; keep up the good work."

Since the lead goose faces the brunt of the wind, the geese flying behind bark out expressions of encouragement to keep the morale up. When the lead goose gets tired, it rotates back into formation and another goose takes the lead, like tag-team partners.

What a beautiful example of the give-and-take of encouragement. I believe encouraging others is one of the greatest things a person can do. But the truth is, those who encourage others often need encouragement themselves.

Moses needed the help of Aaron and Hur when he became exhausted (Exodus 17:12). Even Jesus needed help carrying his cross when he fell beneath its weight (Luke 23:26).

Years ago, as a young, discouraged minister, I wondered if I had what it takes to be a successful evangelist. I was enrolled, at that time, in an internship program designed to help me decide if this was the right path for me or not. My supervising pastor, Ron Treadway, sat across the desk from me and talked with me like a father talks with his son.

"If you remain humble, God is going to take you to big places. You are anointed. You are called. You are gifted," he said as I sat there bug-eyed and baffled. "You've got great parents who have raised you right, and you've got your head screwed on straight. All you have to do now is prepare yourself: stay in the Word, spend time in prayer, and listen to the Holy Spirit."

"Yes, sir," I said as I swallowed the frog in my throat.

"And one more thing. As a young man, you will face all kinds of temptations; keep your eyes on Jesus."

That was almost forty years ago, and I still remember that pep talk because it came at a time when I needed it the most.

Let me encourage you today by saying: "Thanks for all you've done. Thank you, moms and dads, for staying up late to help your kids with homework. Thank you, wives, for getting up early to iron a shirt and bag a lunch. Thank you, husbands, for working overtime so the family could go on vacation. Thank you, co-worker, for doing the routine tasks day after day when no one recognized your hard work. Thank you, son and daughter, for patiently caring for your elderly parent. Thank you, grandparent, for seeing potential in your grandchild when no one else did. Thank you, my friend, for forgiving the spouse that broke your heart. Thank you for pushing forward when you felt like giving up. Thank you for helping others when you were hurting more than they were. Although you've been overlooked and underappreciated, you have worked harder and sacrificed more than your fair share. You belong in heaven's Hall of Fame."

And there's one more thing I want to say, "Quack, quack, quack, honk, honk!" That's goose talk for, "Job well done, keep soaring."

Bear one another's burdens,
and thereby fulfill the law of Christ.
(GALATIANS 6:2 NASB)

EIGHTY-TWO

Put Your Shoes On

Most of the men I know can get by with a few pairs of shoes: something black, something brown, one casual, one dressy, and maybe a pair of boots. For most of the women I know, that's a different story. It's going to take more than a few.

The world of women's shoes is unexplored territory for most men: color selections galore, heel designs of every sort, open toes, closed toes, flats, sandals, bows, straps, buckles, pumps, stilettos, wedges, and platforms.

But let me tell you about the best shoes in the world. They can't be found at the shoe store. Amazon doesn't offer them either. They were given to me as a gift, custom-made by the Divine Cobbler. I didn't know God was in the shoe business until he gave me these shoes. I've had them nearly forty years and they're still good as new.

"For shoes, put on the peace that comes from the Good News so that you will be fully prepared" (Ephesians 6:15 NLT).

With these shoes, you can walk through the valley of the shadow of death and fear no evil (Psalm 23:4). You can trample on serpents and scorpions (Luke 10:19). You can scale the tallest mountain (Habakkuk 3:19). The shoes of peace have non-slip soles (Psalm 73:2) and steel-toed protection (Psalm 91:12). Owners of these shoes have the right to claim the ground they walk on as their own territory (Joshua 1:3).

I wore the shoes of peace through my turbulent adolescent years and made it out unscathed. I wore them on my wedding day, and I'm still happily married three decades later. I've worn the shoes of peace to the cemetery several times. They help me put one foot in front of the other and keep on moving. Last year, I wore the shoes of peace through a global pandemic, and I'm still standing to tell the story. I found out the shoes of peace wear best on rough roads, in dark alleys, and in lonely places.

Oh, did I mention, these shoes are hand-me-downs. They are pre-owned. They once belonged to a carpenter in Nazareth. He walked on water with these shoes. He stood before kings and sat with publicans and sinners while wearing these shoes. He waltzed into no-man's-land (Samaria) to offer these shoes to a desperate woman, and he marched through Jericho to offer them to a blind beggar.

He wore these shoes in the garden of Gethsemane, on the via dolorosa, and up Mount Calvary. But he doesn't need them anymore. You do.

"I am leaving you with a gift—peace of mind and heart. And the peace I give is a gift the world cannot give. So don't be troubled or afraid" (John 14:27 NLT).

I visited the Cobbler's shop this morning, and he told me to tell you that your shoes are ready for pickup. "But I didn't order any shoes," you say. That's right. He ordered them for you. They're a gift. The Cobbler's son paid for them, and if they're like my shoes, you're going to love them. The shoes of peace that once belonged to Jesus, now belong to you. So put your shoes on. You're going places.

Your desire to tell the good news about peace
should be like shoes on your feet.
(EPHESIANS 6:15 CEV)

EIGHTY-THREE

Dramamine

I don't fly much, but when I do, Dramamine is a must. Someone named it correctly: drama mine. Yes sirree. That's what happens if I don't take it before leaving the tarmac. Turbulence in the air leads to turbulence everywhere: swimmy head, queasy stomach, sweaty palms, and jittery bladder.

Sitting at the gate in San Antonio, we were scheduled to fly to Memphis and then on to Richmond, but there was a mechanical problem. I popped a Dramamine in my mouth and prayed for the mechanic. About that time, they made a public announcement explaining our plane needed a replacement part. They didn't have the part in San Antonio, so they asked us to get on the plane, fly to Detroit, install the part, then fly to Memphis.

Excuse me? Did they say fly to Detroit to get the part? How far can eyes bulge without rolling down your face? Let's just say, I needed more than Dramamine. I needed eye surgery, and all the grace heaven could give. Every creak and pop sent me into a tailspin. I don't remember how long the flight was, but that's how long I prayed: every minute, every breath.

By the time we landed in Detroit, no flights were available. We had to spend the night and catch an early flight to Richmond the next morning. They told us our seats had been upgraded to first class. First class? That's the domain of dignitaries and diplomats. My eyes bulged again. This time for good reason. I could hardly wait to fly up front and pretend to be head honcho for the day.

The seat was Cadillac comfy and covered with all the bells and whistles. I whispered, through the crack between the seats, to our friends sitting in front of us, "Hey, I've got two cup holders, ear pods, a television, and a footrest big enough for all four of us."

The executive hotshot across the aisle rolled his eyes at us like we were hillbillies in Hollywood. He didn't say it, but I could read his mind, "How'd I get stuck beside Mr. and Mrs. Neanderthal?"

185

The stewardess catered to our every whim. We had priority access to the lavatory, to free snacks, free drinks, free breakfast, free magazines, free Wi-Fi, free pillows, free blankets, free back massage, free pedicure, free teeth whitening, and free liposuction. (Well, I exaggerated a little, but not much.)

I got so caught up in my newfound benefits, I forgot to take Dramamine, but it didn't matter. My change of perspective had lifted me above my fear of flying.

Life is full of turbulence. Always has been, always will be. Here's a short list: Undeniable diagnosis, unplanned pregnancies, unforgiving relationships, unforeseeable separation, and unpredictable bereavement.

Who said these were friendly skies? They were wrong. Life is fraught with peril and pain, disillusionment and disappointment, misery and misfortune. But I've learned a little secret: The right perspective goes a long way toward turning jitters into joys.

Years ago the Apostle Paul wrote a prescription for anxiety disorder. It's still good for today. Take two tablets, and call me in the morning. (1) "Don't worry about anything." (2) "Pray about everything." Are there any side effects? You betcha. "Then you will experience God's peace" (Philippians 4:6-7 NLT).

We're all on the same flight, dealing with the same turbulence. Some fly in chaos, others fly in calm. It has nothing to do with the weather outside. It has everything to do with the perspective inside.

Fluff your pillow. Prop your feet. Don your sleeping goggles. Trust the Pilot. You'll be home before you know it.

The God of peace will be with you.
(PHILIPPIANS 4:9 NLT)

EIGHTY-FOUR

The Last Supper

Jesus passed portions of food around the table for a meal that would later be known as the Last Supper. Each disciple took a piece of lamb, a sprig of herbs, a cake of figs, and a morsel of unleavened bread. The room was noticeably quiet, except for the casual brush of elbows and the cautious hush of whispers.

The circle of friends had met together in an upper room to celebrate Passover one day early, at the suggestion of their Master. (Tomorrow would be too late; by then, he'd be in Roman chains.) The sun had set behind the hills of Judea, shrouding Jerusalem in the cover of night. Oil lamps glowed on the table, illuminating the face of Jesus, the unkempt beard of Peter, and the charcoal eyes of Judas.

He spoke with passion as he rehearsed the events of the first Passover in Egypt. His disciples had heard the story over and over, but he told it like it was the first time.

"The bitter herbs we eat tonight," Jesus said, "remind us of the bitter hardships of our ancestors." He dipped them in a bowl of vinegar, paused, and spoke of Joseph's coat dipped in blood, the act that inaugurated the nation's bondage in Egypt. He dipped the herbs a second time, paused again, and spoke of the hyssop Moses used to smear the doorpost with blood. Then Jesus ate his herbs and they followed his example. Thirteen men, at the same time, tasted the bitter hardships of Israel. Twelve of them reflected on the bitter past, but one of them thought about the bitter night ahead: a kiss of betrayal, a public denial, and a mock trial.

With bitterness still sharp on his tongue, Jesus blurted out, "One of you at the table will betray me." Heads cocked. Eyes darted. Fingers pointed. Who would do such a thing? They began accusing one another, so Jesus rose from the table and removed his robe. With a towel in one hand and a bowl of water in the other, he washed their feet, and it changed their attitudes from scrutiny to surrender. Then he returned to the table and prepared for the next course.

He lifted the unleavened bread high enough for all to see, like a serpent on a pole. "This is the bread of affliction." He spoke of its life-giving qualities, then pulled it into pieces. "This is my body which is given for you: this do in remembrance of me" (Luke 22:19 KJV). Judas rolled his eyes in silent disgust. (Can't we just eat the Passover like everyone else? Why all the drama?) His eyes stopped rolling at a glimmer of light on the cheek of Jesus. Within hours, those same cheeks would glisten again—with the kiss of a coward in the light of the moon. Jesus dipped the bread and gave it to him. "Do it quickly." The cryptic message was only meant for the traitor. He swallowed the bread, scampered to his feet, and stepped outside into the darkness of night.

Twelve disciples had eaten the bread of affliction, but only eleven would drink the cup of redemption. Jesus swirled the wine under his nose, releasing its fragrance into the air. "This is My blood of the new covenant, which is shed for many for the remission of sins" (Matthew 26:28). They drank together in unison, then sang a song in harmony. Their camaraderie had been restored, at least for a few more hours.

The infamous night of suffering was upon him. Gethsemane waited in the shadows. Jesus knew what was coming: the mob's search on Olivet, Judas's kiss in the garden, and Peter's denial by the fire. He knew his disciples would forsake him before the night was over, yet he treated them as loyal companions until the last morsel was eaten and the last drop was drunk. He dined with Peter in spite of the looming denial. He washed Andrew's feet, knowing he would run away when he needed him the most. Why? Because he loved them, and because he knew this moment of failure was not their undoing. He would eat with them again. He was already planning their next meal together—a messianic banquet in the halls of heaven. For now, he looked beyond their faults. Later, he would look them in the eye and love them just the same.

Jesus feels the same way about you. Don't believe me? You should. He's holding a place for you at the banquet table, and he won't start the party until you get there.

He loved them to the end.
(JOHN 13:1)

EIGHTY-FIVE

The Glance of Grace

Three public denials, two rooster crows, and one dark night is all it took to turn Peter's world inside out and upside down. But a single glance of grace put it all back together again.

He still had the smell of smoke in his hair when his face blushed as red as the embers at his feet. Start your stopwatch when Peter opens his mouth and swears, "I don't know the man" (Matthew 26:72 NIV). Stop your stopwatch when Jesus drops his head in disappointment. It took all of two seconds for a three-year friendship to go up in smoke. But a look of love from the eyes of Jesus sparked a ray of hope in the soul of Peter.

The contrasts on that night couldn't be greater. While Jesus was inside Caiaphas's house, Peter was outside in the courtyard. Jesus was under fire; Peter was warming himself by the fire. Jesus stood among interrogators; Peter sat among captors. Jesus was on trial in a kangaroo court; Peter was under the watch of a barnyard rooster. Jesus stood strong under pressure from powerful men; Peter buckled under gentle suggestions of a servant girl. Jesus identified himself as the Son of God, and Peter denied he ever knew him. One spoke the truth, the other told a lie.

Let's revisit that unforgettable moment. It was a dark night in Jerusalem, and the dirty deed taking place behind closed doors made it even darker. Sanhedrin members slipped out of their cozy beds and sneaked to the high priest's house under cover of night. They were looking for a loophole. The One they hated most was in chains, and if they could find two agreeable witnesses, he'd soon be on the cross. It didn't take long for the witch hunt to turn into a free-for-all.

Caiaphas's sprawling palace sat atop Mount Zion, close to the Temple. Marble columns supported porticos. Reflective pools graced the landscape. And on that particular night, a charcoal fire lit up the center of the courtyard. It cast its amber glow on the faces of chilled servants and one timid turncoat who followed Jesus at a distance.

Peter sat down by the fire. He rubbed his cold hands together and tried to blend in with the crowd, but the blue-collar fisherman couldn't hide among the officers of the court.

Crickets chirped. Fire crackled. Servants shuffled. Then one of them noticed the outsider. "You also were with Jesus of Galilee" (Matthew 26:69 NIV). Peter's blood pressure spiked as his integrity sank. "I don't know what you're talking about." He tried to sound persuasive, but his accent betrayed him. He was from "Hick Town," Galilee, and they knew it. Peter wasn't a good liar. He tried three different times, but it never worked. He raised his voice, they weren't convinced. He raised his right hand and swore. They knew he was lying. His darting eyes and pursed lips gave him away.

How ironic that God used a rooster, the king of chickens, to convince Peter he was acting like a chicken.

Caiaphas's officers handed Jesus over to Roman guards, who transported him to Pilate's judgment hall. In the purplish orange of morning light, Peter heard the convoy march through the courtyard. He looked north, Jesus looked south, and their eyes met in the middle. "Then Peter remembered" (Luke 22:61 NIV).

I hope he remembered more than Christ's words at the Last Supper, the prediction of his denial. I hope Peter remembered the day Jesus borrowed his boat, the day the fish nets broke, the day his mother-in-law was healed, and the day Jesus rescued him from drowning. I hope Peter remembered Jesus saying, "You are Peter, and on this rock I will build My church" (Matthew 16:18).

Whatever Peter remembered, it was the beginning of his restoration. Peter left the compound and found a solitary place to pray. He wept. He cried. He moaned. He groaned.

Then he remembered again. He remembered that look in the eyes of Jesus—not a look of condemnation, but a look of grace. And that one glance of grace was enough to sustain Peter for the days ahead: days of crucifixion and burial, days of resurrection and ascension, days of persecution and imprisonment. It's the same glance that sustains us today. Look up. Christ is looking down. See it? It's the glance of grace.

And the Lord turned and looked at Peter.
(LUKE 22:61)

EIGHTY-SIX

I'm Thirsty

*M*om, I'm thirsty," the three-year-old cried out in the middle of the night. His voice pierced the darkness. Mary rolled out of bed, trying not to wake Joseph. She wrapped a shawl around her shoulders, lit an oil lamp, and tiptoed across the cold floor.

"Mom, I'm thirsty," little Jesus said again.

She poured water from a pitcher into a small cup, yawned, and sat down on the edge of his mat. "Here. Be careful." She cupped her hands around his as he pulled the cup to his lips. He slurped it down and handed her the empty cup. Mary wiped away a stray drop of water trickling down his chin, kissed him on the nose, and whispered, "Now go back to sleep and don't wet the bed."

Twenty-seven years later, Jesus sat down on the rim of Jacob's well. It was high noon and he was thirsty. His disciples were nowhere in sight, but a woman of Sychar was headed straight for him. She had a clay pot on one shoulder and a length of rope in her opposite hand. As soon as she arrived at the well, Jesus blurted out, "Give me something to drink." She froze in her tracks and raised both Samaritan eyebrows. "Please," he said. "I'm so thirsty."

Six months later, Jesus and his disciples topped the Mount of Olives on their way to Bethany. Sweat trailed down their backs. A lizard darted between their feet and hid in the shade of a rock. It was a midsummer scorcher, but Jesus pressed on. He knew water was just ahead. At last, the exhausted travelers knocked on Martha's door. "Would you like some hot bread? It's fresh out of the oven."

Jesus cleared his throat, "No, but I sure am thirsty."

The following year, Jesus and his disciples went to Jerusalem for the Feast of Tabernacles. Crowds gathered, Levites sang, and priests offered sacrifices. To everyone's surprise, Jesus scooped two handfuls of water from the Pool of Siloam and shouted, "If you are thirsty, come to me and drink!" (John 7:37 CEV).

A year and a half later, Jesus hung on a cross, suspended between heaven and earth. His ankles were shattered, his hands punctured, his back lacerated, and his brow pierced. Dark circles formed under his eyes. His blood pressure dropped. His lungs wheezed. He finally managed a few words. Not the expected three words, "I am thirsty," but only two words, "I thirst" (John 19:28 KJV). To save a word was to save a breath.

His mouth was dry, his lips were parched, and his throat was raspy. His last swallow of liquid had been in the upper room at dinner with his disciples, twenty hours earlier. The Roman soldiers never thought to offer him a drink. Why would they? He was a dead man walking.

The days when his mother fetched him a cup of cool water were long gone. Jacob's well and Martha's kitchen were distant memories. The Pool of Siloam was out of view, on the other side of the city wall.

"I thirst," he groaned from the cross. A soldier pressed a sponge onto the end of a hyssop branch, dunked it in a jar of vinegar, and lifted it to the lips of Jesus. His bitter death was toasted with a sour drink. It moves my heart to think about it. His final taste of earth was not sweet wine; it was sour vinegar. Why?

So he could share your sour experiences and offer you a better hope—a seat beside him on the bank of a river, the River of Life.

Come, all you who are thirsty, come to the waters.
(Isaiah 55:1 NIV)

EIGHTY-SEVEN

Do You Belong to Jesus?

Come with me, if you dare, to a ghoulish place not intended for human eyes. It's right over here, beyond this veil of darkness. I've been granted permission to bring one visitor. Are you up to it?"

You give a half-hearted shrug. I take it as a yes. We take two steps forward and slice between the folds of a curtain. Without warning, we find ourselves standing in the realm of evil spirits.

"Shhh!" I touch my finger to my lips. "Don't make a sound. If they see us, we won't get out of here alive."

The ground looks the same as always, but gravity has no hold on us. We hover in the air at the speed of thought. It's nightfall in Jerusalem. The temple gates are closed. A candle winks in the watchtower. There's a rustle in the bushes.

In the shadows we see a man crawling on all fours, spitting curses and vomiting blasphemy. The limbs of an old tree arch over a thorny gorge. A noose dangles on a branch in the light of the moon.

"That's Judas," I whisper.

"Is he going to hang himself? I'm not watching this."

"Look." I point to two dark figures drawing near. One has hair like Medusa; it crawls with a dozen snakes. The other looks like a prehistoric lizard. He sniffs the air with his forked tongue.

"Don't move a muscle."

You bury your eyes in your hands and pray, "Jesus. Jesus."

It's too late. They see us. Thankfully, they are here for Judas; otherwise we'd have a fight on our hands. Apollyon called the shot. "Drag the betrayer's soul to Hades." These two imps were sent to escort him to the abyss. We watch from a not-so-safe distance.

Imp One: "There's no grace for you now. It's too late. This is the only way out."

Judas shakes his head and lets out a low moan.

Imp Two: "C'mon. Up on your feet."

Judas climbs to his feet and stumbles forward. Once the rope is around his neck, he lets out a woeful sigh. One of the imps gives a final shove as Judas leaps from the embankment and dangles in the night air. A raven perches on his shoulder. The moon hides behind a cloud. A stray dog yelps in the distance.

The soul of Judas escapes his body, and within seconds the imps apprehend him, one on each side. He squirms. He fights. He bucks. All to no avail. A wormhole opens to the underworld, and the three of them vanish out of sight.

"Let's get out of here," you say as you grab my arm.

"Not yet. Wait."

The wormhole opens again, and the same imps appear. This time they glide over the city wall and head west, past the serpent's pool and down through the Hinnom Valley. We float behind them, spying on their next mission. They settle down near a pile of rocks at the lower end of the ravine, and for the second time tonight, we see a man crawling on all fours. He sobs. He wails. He thrashes in the dirt. His long hair hides his face. Dark shadows hide his grief.

Imp One: "There's no grace for you now. It's too late. There's only one way out."

Imp Two: "Here's a flint rock. Slit your wrist. It'll stop the pain."

Lightning bolts from heaven strike the ground with a thud. Your jaw drops. My eyes brighten. Angels surround the man, with swords drawn. They're ten feet tall, steely-eyed, and dressed for battle.

The imps recoil and hiss, "He's ours."

"This one belongs to Jesus," the angel declares.

"No. He denied him three times already."

The angel swings his flashing sword—Shwoosh! "Back off. You know Jesus prayed for him, that his faith wouldn't fail (Luke 22:32, author's paraphrase). Peter is a marked man. He belongs to God."

We hover in the air just above the treetops. "That was what I wanted you to see."

"What? The angels and their flashing swords?"

"No," I say as the imps scamper into the darkness. "What it means to belong to Jesus."

Fear not, for I have redeemed you;
I have called you by your name; You are Mine.
(Isaiah 43:1)

EIGHTY-EIGHT

Easter Morning

There was just enough light coming through the mini blinds to watch the blades on the ceiling fan twirl in the middle of the night. He closed his eyes, but they popped right back open again. His wife lay beside him snoring, in a deep sleep. He thought about taking his life that night. His pistol lay in the nightstand drawer, but he didn't want her to find him in a pool of blood. He loved her too much.

She was a good woman, a church-going woman. She baked cookies to sell at the yard sale and gave the funds to orphans on the Indian Reservation. She invited the neighbors over for dinner just to be hospitable. She read her Bible every morning with her coffee and toast and kissed him goodbye on her way out the door. "I love you," she'd say. But he never looked up from reading the newspaper.

It was Saturday night, April 14, the night before Easter. Perhaps he couldn't sleep because he'd promised to go to church with her the next morning. He hadn't been to church in three Easters. The last time he went, he swore he'd never go back. "Those church folks are a bunch of hypocrites," he said. "I've seen those pompous deacons down at the club with young women. Their wives didn't have a clue where they were. If that's religion, I don't need any." But he knew the difference between real religion and what was fake. The "real deal" was snoring right beside him, and he couldn't deny it.

He looked at the clock. It was 3:00 a.m. Finally, he drifted off to that place where time doesn't matter. The faces in his dream vanished as soon as the alarm clock went off. His wife had it set for 7:00 a.m., to the local Christian channel.

She got up in a flash. "Good morning." It was the day she'd been waiting for. He was going to church with her, and it was an answer to her prayer. He made one excuse after another, trying to wiggle out of his commitment. "I don't have a clean shirt." She held one up on a hanger and smiled. It was pressed and ready to go. "I don't have any decent shoes. Mine are all scuffed up from work." She opened a shoe box and pulled out brand-new shoes, just his size. "But what about breakfast?" he asked.

"I'll have eggs and toast on the table in ten minutes, plus they have coffee and donuts down at the church." She'd thought of everything.

He felt awkward walking into church that day, with all the fake smiles and plastic handshakes. "Where's the men's room if I need to get out of here?" he whispered. She accommodated his every wish, praying all the while under her breath.

It wasn't the choir's singing, nor the pastor's preaching, that got a hold of his heart. It was the skit put on by the youth group. It portrayed a man who couldn't get to Jesus because of all the sinful interferences: a liquor bottle, a drug needle, a stack of money, a lewd woman, and finally, the kicker—a loaded pistol.

Tears flowed down his cheeks. He couldn't take it any longer. He grabbed his wife by the hand and said, "Let's go." She was disappointed that he wanted to leave, but when they reached the center aisle, he headed for the altar, not the door. He fell on his knees and sobbed in both hands. "I'm so sorry for the way I've lived." She clung to his arm and cried tears of joy. It was the answer to a lifetime of prayer.

Today, he teaches a Sunday school class of young boys and leads mission teams to help orphaned kids on the Indian Reservation.

Therefore, my dear brothers and sisters, stand firm.
Let nothing move you. Always give yourselves fully
to the work of the Lord, because you know that
your labor in the Lord is not in vain.
(1 CORINTHIANS 15:58 NIV)

EIGHTY-NINE

The Mysterious Napkin

John saw the vacant tomb first, from a distance, gawking from the gate. He poked his head inside the unclean place but left his sanctified feet on the soil outside. Bent over with his hands on his knees, he peered into the darkness, curious as to the whereabouts of his missing Lord. John respected the scene of the crime. He left no fingerprints, no forensic evidence. As a spectator behind police tape, he showed proper restraint. Only his nose and eyeballs intruded the place of entombment. He dared not trespass the boundaries of the Messiah's morgue.

But Peter is a different animal. Restraint is not a word in his vocabulary. This is the man who stepped out of a boat, defied logic, and walked on water in the thick of night. You know Peter; thinking before acting is not a requirement. He'll yank a sword out of its sheath and whack a man's ear off before you can count to three.

Older and not as fleet of foot, Peter arrived at the tomb second, gulping air and wiping sweat. The agility of his youth had left him in the dust a year ago. He contends with the limitations of age now. A stiff knee. A sore back, A pudgy ring around his waist. He's not the gazelle he once was. He's a raging bull looking for a China shop.

Peter pushed past John and barged into the tomb without a second thought, ready to jump right into the middle of the mystery. His eyes darted every which way, looking for something but finding nothing. His hands rested on his hips as his eyes adjusted to the dark. Still trying to catch his breath, he caught something else, a glimpse of a garment in the corner.

By this time, John had creeped into the shadows and stood beside him dead center in the room. Both of their eyes locked onto the facial napkin at the same time. Separated from the burial clothes, it rested opposite them, on the other side—folded by the corners, pressed flat, and arranged just so. This was not the work of a thief.

What Roman soldier would steal the body of Jesus but take the time to arrange the napkin with such distinction?

The light clicked on for John. A slight smile pushed his fears away. He saw the handiwork of Jesus in the napkin and believed. The same hand that arranged the stars in the sky and placed the sun in its orbit, the same hand that plucked Abram from the Chaldeans and picked David among his seven brothers, and the same hand that touched unclean lepers and smeared blinded eyes with spittle and mud is the same hand that placed this cloth in the corner, on point and on purpose.

It was more than a sign. It was a signature. It was a last-minute note from a divine suitor, a love letter to a betrothed bride. Although he must leave her behind, he cannot leave without a gesture of love. The napkin in the corner was his bouquet on the table, a dozen roses at a doubtful moment. Would his soon-to-be bride feel estranged without his presence? Would she feel jilted, abandoned, or neglected? Would she think he skipped town without a kiss goodbye? Our beloved Lord would never do such a thing. Before stepping out of the tomb and heading off on his merry way, he decided to leave a love note. He didn't have a hammer and chisel to etch a note in stone. He didn't have a quill and parchment to leave a proper post. His only stationary was the burial napkin that had covered his face.

He held it by two corners and shook the wrinkles out. Then he found a smooth place on a rock and spread it out flat. "This is for you, Simon Peter." Jesus folded it once. "This is for you, John." He folded it twice. "And this is for all who will believe." He folded it yet again. At last, he took a step back, blew a kiss, gave a wink, and walked out of the tomb triumphant.

If you had been there, he would have hugged you. Since you weren't, he left you a note. The napkin says, "I'm alive." It says, "I'm thinking about you." It says, "I love you, I'm coming back, and the next time I leave, I'm taking you with me."

Then the other disciple, who came to the tomb first,
went in also; and he saw and believed.
(JOHN 20:8)

NINETY

The Tightrope Walker

The year was 1987. I stood at a postcard rack in a novelty shop, rotating the card display. I pulled one postcard after the other, spellbound at the beauty and mystery of Niagara Falls. From summertime snapshots to images of Niagara's winter wonderland, my admiration and appreciation for the popular tourist spot soared by the moment.

We could hear the constant roar of the falls outside, even though we were inside the gift shop. A few vacationers, including my wife, meandered from aisle to aisle looking for trinkets and souvenirs.

I spun the card rack around one more time and spotted a small booklet on the top shelf. The story I read that day still amazes me, thirty-some years later.

According to eyewitnesses, in 1855, a French tightrope walker named Charles Blondin walked across the falls from the Canadian side to the American side with no safety net underneath.

Then he proceeded to walk across blindfolded, and yet another time, pushing an empty wheelbarrow in front of him. And to trump the previous feats of bravery, he walked across again with a set of stilts under his feet. (He was either courageous or crazy. Maybe a little bit of both.)

But Charles wanted to try something never attempted before, so he asked for a volunteer to ride on his back as he crossed the falls one last time. This would be his grand finale (perhaps in more ways than one).

According to the booklet, no one volunteered. I thought to myself, if I had been there, no one would have volunteered. And if you had been there, no one would have volunteered. Am I right? You betcha I'm right.

Harry Colcord, his manager, accepted the challenge and climbed on Charles Blondin's back.

The daring tightrope walker headed across the misty gorge, one deliberate step at a time, on a wire suspended 160 feet high in the air.

However, halfway across the watery chasm, Charles labored to the point of exhaustion. He told Harry to get off of his back and stand on the rope behind him until he regained strength in his legs.

Let me interrupt the story to say, if he had persuaded me to get on his back, he would have never persuaded me to get off of his back. I would have clung to him like Saran Wrap.

Defying all odds, Harry climbed off Charles's back and stood on the rope behind him. A minute later, he climbed on his back the second time and the two of them crossed safely to the other side. Whew.

I returned the booklet to the card rack and found my wife in the store. "Let me tell you what happened here in 1855."

I've told that story many times since then, and it never gets old. It's the greatest example of trust I've ever read. To trust a man with your life to the point of riding on his back across Niagara Falls, with no safety net underneath, is beyond my wildest imagination.

What could be more valuable than your life? Only one thing—your soul. Who can you trust with the salvation of your soul? Only one man. His name is not Charles, it's Jesus. He has proven himself over and over. His reputation is spotless. His promises are failproof. He's never dropped a single soul, though he has crossed the chasm of death many times.

Whether it's Niagara Falls with its crashing water or the Jordan River with its chilly tide, Jesus can get you safely to the other side. You are secure in his arms.

When you take your final breath, and life on earth succumbs to life eternal, your flight from terra firma to celestial glory will be accompanied by your nail-scarred Savior.

You don't have to be afraid to die. He has already transported millions of souls to heaven before you, and he will carry you safely to the other side as well. You trusted him at the cross. Now trust him at the crossing.

I know whom I have believed and am persuaded that He is
able to keep what I have committed to Him until that Day.
(2 TIMOTHY 1:12)

Endnotes

CHAPTER 6
1. John Newton, "Amazing Grace." 1779, Public Domain

CHAPTER 9
1. "Ellicott's Commentary for English Reader's," *Bible Hub, https://biblehub.com/commentaries/judges/3-31.htm* (July 30, 2021).

CHAPTER 13
1. "Strong's Hebrew 4036: Magor-missabib = 'terror on every side,'" *Bible Hub, https://biblehub.com/strongs/jeremiah/20-3.htm* (July 30, 2021).

CHAPTER 19
1. Isaiah G. Martin, "The Eastern Gate." 1905, Public Domain

CHAPTER 22
1. "Strong's Hebrew 8095: Simeon or Shimeon = 'heard,'" *Bible Hub, https://biblehub.com/strongs/genesis/49-5.htm* (July 30, 2021)

CHAPTER 25
1. "In flagrante delicto (Latin: 'in blazing offence')," *Wikipedia, The Free Encyclopedia, https://en.wikipedia.org/wiki/In_flagrante_delicto* (July 30, 2021).

CHAPTER 37
1. Warren D. Cornell and Oliver W. Cooper, "Wonderful Peace." 1892, Public Domain.

CHAPTER 39
1. C. S. Hamilton and T. P. Hamilton, "I Am Determined to Hold Out," 1900, Public Domain.

CHAPTER 49

1. Richard J. Foster, *Freedom of Simplicity: Finding Harmony in a Complex World*, Revised edition. HarperOne Publishers, 2010. Kindle edition.

2. Anna Bartlett Warner, "Jesus Loves Me," 1859, Public Domain.

CHAPTER 64

1. Charlotte Elliot, "Just As I Am," 1835, Public Domain.

CHAPTER 78

1. Fanny Crosby, "Praise Him! Praise Him!" 1869, Public Domain.

Topical Index

BIBLE CHARACTERS

CHRISTMAS

HOLY WEEK

Scripture References

FOR ADDITIONAL COPIES OF

THE *Storyteller's*
DEVOTIONAL
VOLUME TWO

PLEASE ORDER @ AMAZON.COM

Also Available @ Amazon.com is
Clifton West's first book,

THE *Storyteller's* DEVOTIONAL

If you have questions, comments, or would like
to leave a review, please contact the author:

Clifton West
6100 Surrywood Drive
Prince George, Virginia 23875

Email: CWest1964@gmail.com

Made in the USA
Middletown, DE
20 October 2022